TAROT
THERAPY

TAROT
THERAPY

Harness the Healing
Power of the Deck

LEONA NICHOLE BLACK

ST. MARTIN'S
ESSENTIALS
NEW YORK

The information in this book is not intended to replace the advice of the reader's own physician or other medical professional. You should consult a medical professional in matters relating to health, especially if you have existing medical conditions, and before starting, stopping, or changing the dose of any medication you are taking. Individual readers are solely responsible for their own health-care decisions. The author and the publisher do not accept responsibility for any adverse effects individuals may claim to experience, whether directly or indirectly, from the information contained in this book.

Published in the United States by St. Martin's Essentials,
an imprint of St. Martin's Publishing Group

TAROT THERAPY. Copyright © 2023 by Leona Nichole Black.
All rights reserved. Printed in the United States of America.
For information, address St. Martin's Publishing Group,
120 Broadway, New York, NY 10271.

www.stmartins.com

The Library of Congress Cataloging-in-Publication Data is available upon request.

ISBN 978-1-250-88646-0 (trade paperback)
ISBN 978-1-250-88647-7 (ebook)

Our books may be purchased in bulk for promotional, educational,
or business use. Please contact your local bookseller or the Macmillan Corporate
and Premium Sales Department at 1-800-221-7945, extension 5442,
or by email at MacmillanSpecialMarkets@macmillan.com.

Originally published in the UK by Orion Spring
First St. Martin's Essentials trade paperback edition: 2023

10 9 8 7 6 5 4 3 2 1

With thanks to:

*my tarot clients who have trusted me to participate
in the beautification of their lives*

and

*the friends and family who have orbited
around me like moons, reflecting back my light
during my darkest times*

CONTENTS

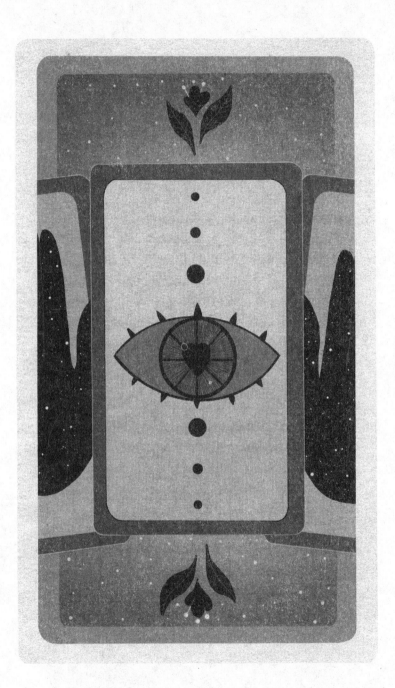

WHAT IS
TAROT THERAPY?

I first came across tarot readings on YouTube almost ten years ago. Tarot wasn't mainstream at that time; it was building in popularity but was still very niche. A popular tarot video then would have received maybe 2,000 views, in contrast to 150,000 and more for some of the bigger names today. Tarot wasn't something that was spoken about day-to-day either. It existed minimally in occult TV shows, and I had a friend who had a "woman they went to" to predict the future, but it was still very obscure.

The more I watched tarot videos, the more I found myself charmed by mothers who were doing readings for the pleasure of sharing, fitting them in around their otherwise busy work and family schedules. I would fall asleep to a tarot video as if listening to a lullaby and wake up and listen to another while I got dressed for work. Watching tarot was one of my favorite things to do with my downtime. Today, I wouldn't recommend listening to so many tarot readings in a short period of time. In those beginning stages I was falling in love, and you know how it is in those early giddy stages when it feels like there is no such thing as too much.

I loved seeing the different decks and art styles. The ways the creators illustrated the highs and lows of life. How they imagined love or grief, or endurance, or triumph. I was soothed by hearing these women gently describe the difficulties of adult life and offer hope. I liked being given tarot predictions for the drama of the upcoming week and then living through it thinking, *Gosh, I'm so glad I had a heads-up. I can handle things differently.* After months of watching as much tarot as I could, I realized it was not because I wanted to hear a tarot reading but because I was longing for my own relationship with the cards. I wanted to practice.

HOW I GOT STARTED

Today, years on from when I first started practicing, many of my clients are open and enthusiastic when I recommend they get a deck of tarot cards of their own. This wasn't always the case. In the earlier days, people were curious enough to try a tarot reading but reluctant to work with a deck of their own. Perhaps through lack of knowledge and confidence, or skepticism, but sometimes because of cultural experiences that discouraged it. I could relate to this because I also grappled with fears and questions about using tarot, and so it was a slow journey to me buying my first deck.

I struggled with my religious upbringing and was generally apprehensive about the unknowns of what tarot could open me up to. Would I start to experience strange and uncanny things that belong only in ghost novels and films because I was playing with something I shouldn't? Even though I was uncertain, I couldn't deny that it was working; it was improving my life. So, as my birthday approached, I bought myself a set of cards and the rest is history.

At first, I was very literal, intellectual, and practical about it. Tarot was no different to me than a daily motivational message. The guidance could have just as easily come from a book of quotes or my favorite writer's monthly newsletter. I didn't want to go too far into the mysticism of it all (that would come later). Tarot for me at that time was for practical down-to-earth advice, and the deck was simply a graphic alphabet system. A way of writing my own story.

Just a couple of months after getting my first deck, my next "first" was a solo trip to Florence, Italy, a place with a long history of cartomancy (using playing cards for life insights and fortune telling). I spent slow days on trains along the beautiful western coast, reading books about the tarot suit system and traditional meanings of the cards. I began to memorize the different characters, themes, and scenarios. I remember being full of apprehension at the start of the trip on my way to the airport, thinking that I was pushing myself too far out of my comfort zone by going alone to a place I had never been to before and where I did not speak the language. But that trip became a beautiful origin point to where years later, long periods of solo travel would come to define my spiritual journey and day-to-day life.

Back home, after reading tarot for myself for a few months, I began doing short readings for friends, and then for members of the Black feminist society at my university where I was president at the time. The beautiful feedback I received and the sense of direction and clarity tarot was bringing to my own life gave me confidence. I came to love tarot, and now, even when I'm at my most tired or when I've taken months off from reading for others, it has been a consistent source of beauty, pleasure, and care.

My love for tarot brought me to a fork in the road. I was years into my PhD research, and around the time when I should have been finishing my third higher education degree, I was conflicted by wanting a change in direction. I was burned out by academia and I didn't want to write long theoretical papers anymore. I wanted to take my gift for abstract thought and use it to support my community with tarot readings around the same themes I had been researching and writing about all my life. I wanted to move from *thinking* to *being* in the practice of joy and healing, and exploring ways to create liberating life changes for whole communities, using spiritual tools and practices to move around the limitations of structural inequalities. I wanted practical and relatable approaches so that even people with very limited resources and support could find a method of change, instead of success and the overcoming of obstacles being the inspiring story of just a lucky few who made it up from the bottom. I wanted this especially for the communities I belonged to, and this was how Tarot Therapy was born: out of my desire to bring healing to people being harmed and disadvantaged by long-standing social issues.

Today, I never travel far away from home without at least one deck in my bag. A few weeks ago it took me thirty minutes to re-box and pack away all the cards that were sprawled across the living room floor as I sought to coach myself through a difficult weekend. Picking cards and laying them out in spreads like a math equation, giving my stress and my questions a place to go. Now I can't imagine ever again struggling through the challenges of life disoriented, confused, and alone. I can't imagine not having a perspective to root my hope in. I can't imagine not having the cryptic empathy of seeing my mental and emotional state unfold as a story in front of me one card at a time. I can't imagine not living with the peace that comes from the wise counsel of a Tarot Therapy practice.

WHAT IS THE TAROT?

The tarot is a form of cartomancy where a pack of illustrated cards—typically seventy-eight—is used for divination (reading symbols within a defined meaning system to predict future events and/or illuminate hidden knowledge). There is much conjecture about the origins of the tarot. But we do know that the standardized tarot illustration system that is most used and adapted is by British-born, and of Jamaican descent, illustrator Pamela Colman

Smith, who in 1909 created the imagery that is so widely used now, alongside occult writer Arthur Edward Waite.

A tarot deck is divided into twenty-two major arcana, which are archetypes representing universal themes of human experience, and fifty-six minor arcana as a more detailed exploration of how those archetypes show up in day-to-day life. The minor arcana are also divided into suits with elemental correspondences: Wands (Fire), Pentacles (Earth), Swords (Air), and Cups (Water). Each suit and element informs the meaning of the card. For example, the Wands suit can symbolize instinct and action; the Swords suit can be psyche or changeability. Each suit in the minor arcana includes Court Cards (King, Queen, Knight, and Page) as characters that represent either us as the subject of the reading, or other people who are influencing our lives. When pulling tarot cards, the different card combinations that are pulled in response to a question tell a story of our lives. They can contextualize the past and give indication of what may come in the future as a consequence of the present.

I have always been a deeply introspective person and when I started to read the tarot I had already seen a psychiatrist for suicidal ideation and been in four years of talk therapy. I had been invested in working on my mental health and well-being for years. As an intellectual working and studying in a university, my whole life was about questioning, and this made my approach to tarot distinct from the fortune-telling brand of its occult associations. I was interested in using the tarot to become *well*. Tarot became an adaptive therapeutic process because of the way

I chose to use it, and the training I had in asking beneficial and constructive questions was key.

The tarot is a tool for intuition, and we need our intuition whenever we want to navigate life beyond the obvious physical appearance of things, because there is more to life than meets the eye. Our intuition is like another sense (like smell or taste) that helps us organize our experiences of the world. We sometimes misguidedly expect our intuition to be a perfect voice of inner wisdom just waiting to be listened to. But intuition has to be grown and developed and our ability to understand sacred truths has to be built up over time through learning and experience. The mechanisms of our intuition—namely our psychic skill—have to be honed and without doing this we are not very wise at all. Without practice, the intuition can be crude, underdeveloped, and clumsy. We may have dramatic moments where we feel a strong push away from or toward something, that we later note as intuitive wisdom. At other times we may get no sense of direction at all. Or feel that we trusted an intuitive nudge or urge and ended up worse off. A misfire.

Our intuition is comprised of our "clair" talents such as: clairsentience—empathic feeling, receiving information through emotions (this is one of my most developed gifts); clairvoyance—receiving information through visions, often prophetic, but can relate to people or places in the past or present; clairaudience—to hear messages and sounds, not dependent on the ears (mediums for example may use this skill for conversations with spirits); and the list of abilities goes on.

Our intuition is strengthened when we practice using our spiritual senses in day-to-day life. The tarot is then a very helpful practical tool for developing our intuition. This is because we get regular feedback by the results we see in our daily lives. Regular tarot practice helps us hone our intuitive senses. For example, let's say you pull a card to indicate the energy of the day ahead and get The Sun. You interpret that card as a sign of optimism and positivity; however, you have the worst day possible—you lose something important, and you receive nonstop bad news. Understandably, you question the reading, and hopefully, with some maturity, your interpretation too. Was it a card indicating a positive and happy day, or perhaps a message about illumination, news, and things coming to light? This is where your intuitive skill comes in. As a clairsentient tarot reader I could pull The Sun card and also feel a sense of overwhelm when holding it, and this would shape my interpretation of the symbolism of The Sun. Just that small additional piece of intuitive knowledge makes me a more skillful reader and gives me more accurate reading abilities.

Anybody can *use* cards for whatever purpose they choose, but not everybody has the talent for reading or divining with cards. I have some clients who read tarot for themselves and book tarot appointments with me to get a perspective that points out any blind spots they may have; to strengthen and validate their intuition through confirmation of what they are sensing; and to receive spiritual teaching and instruction from me. On the other hand, I have other clients who don't read cards at all and only ever engage with the tarot as a listener. The same choice is posed to you as a reader of this book:

- You have the choice to use a tarot deck alongside the discussion as part of a therapeutic self-recovery process, by going through the questioning exercises in each chapter and pulling cards. (See page 16, "How to Work with This Book.")
- Even if you don't have a tarot deck you can do the Tarot Therapy practice by exploring the exercises with your friends, community, or therapist. You might find it useful to write down your thoughts and findings in a notebook or on your phone.
- Alternatively, you can explore this book without taking the further steps of the exercises, instead enjoying the journey as a curious student learning from my wisdom as an experienced Tarot Therapy practitioner.

WHAT IS TAROT THERAPY?

Tarot Therapy is a practice of deepening and strengthening our most important relationship: the one we have with ourselves. It is a mirror of our soul, or psyche, our persona. Unlike common tarot practice, it places less emphasis on predicting the future; Tarot Therapy is instead about our quality of experience in the present, as a pivotal factor in what we hope to come next. The emphasis of Tarot Therapy is addressing the disruption of hostility and fear in our lives. Whether that's from our environment (work, home, family, etc.) or the muddled condition of our mind. It is creating safety by exposing harm—from others or as forms of self-neglect—and understanding its causes. The questioning ethos of Tarot Therapy is exploring possibilities to remove and remedy spiritual, mental, and emotional injury, leaving room for us to heal and recover.

Tarot Therapy as a regular practice, sometimes as often as daily, helps to strengthen our resolve in the principles that lead to our healing by repeating the messaging in different ways. I do weekly Tarot Therapy live streams for my House of Black community and this is something I say often; that we will get the same message in different ways until we are ready to move on to something else. The tarot card Five of Pentacles comes up frequently as we work through the themes of personal hardship, enduring a pandemic, loneliness, etc. The presence of that card and its position in relation to other tarot cards in the reading helps us chart our journey in dealing with those challenges.

Tarot Therapy is a dialogue between the reader and the deck using the voice of our intuition. It is an immersive experience where we cease rationalizing away the wisdom of our imagination and build trust in our perceptions. For example, you shuffle and select the tarot card The Empress. The wheat field illustration in the background of her throne catches your attention this time and you recall the themes of autumn and harvest. You start to think of your creative process and the need to value your work and be sustained by all that you have produced thus far. Or maybe you are considering a remortgage and the themes of harvest give you peace about withdrawing some equity and reinvesting in yourself. There are many possibilities because the tarot is not binary—we limit ourselves when we think in extremes and expect absolutes. It is an imaginative story you are telling yourself and, at times, you are hearing from a narrator with a much bigger vision than you.

Tarot Therapy then is for mental clarity and emotional recovery. This implies that there may be times when we come to the practice hurt, distressed, or confused. But even when we aren't in the best possible mental state for contemplating our circumstances, there is still a benefit to the practice. Sometimes that comes by pulling cards and seeing the picture of exactly what we feel at that time. By giving voice to our pain and language to our emotions. Sometimes it can be clarifying when we aren't sure what is disturbing our peace; this is one of the most profound aspects of tarot and I love supporting my clients in this way. Anyone can say, "I'm sorry this happened to you," but someone with no former or intimate knowledge of your circumstances laying out an illustration of your life and feelings is like a beautiful form of cosmic validation. It is a way that we feel seen and heard. Even when you are alone with your deck of cards, that experience can be very comforting. From there, when we are ready to, we can interrogate—why, how, what could bring change?

To choose to do Tarot Therapy is to be in conversation with yourself and others. It is broadening your perspective by developing trusted counsel and guidance. It is finding companionship and being acknowledged in your life experiences. It is being protected and celebrated. Disciplined and cautioned. It is consciously playing a role in your ongoing transformation.

CAN TAROT REALLY BE THERAPY?

It is common to hear that a tarot reading cannot replace going to talk therapy and I do agree with this—to an extent. Tarot reveals. Its value is to show you what is happening and what is possible. But the healing and personal transformation work is in the choices we make when we have packed away the cards. Tarot is generally diagnostic—the "what." I am frequently told by clients that I have been able to share truths with them in a single reading that took years for them to come to in talk therapy. This is a regular occurrence for me in my personal practice, having breakthrough moments and realizations about myself and my actions. This is very powerful, but still, that is often where a reading will end. A skillful reader may be able to tell you how to make changes but that is generally where the relationship between reader and client stops. Talk therapy can be part of the *process* of figuring out how to make those advised changes as something you live out day-to-day. Though a spiritual counseling approach to tarot where we work together at regular intervals is something I have offered over the years, the majority of people use tarot readings as a one-off service a few times a year. So, it is fair to say, when approached in this way tarot is not therapeutic, it is advisory.

This however does not mean that tarot *cannot* be therapy, and there is a cultural bias in the suggestion that talk therapy is inherently more valuable, useful, or effective than engaging a tarot practice for healing. While I have found talk therapy incredibly transformative, the growing trend of recommending therapy to everyone as a coverall "get help" message can compromise our emotional safety and deepen alienation. Therapists are not supremely capable and virtuous. They are all working within the boundaries of their own cultural biases and sociopolitical values. For example, even while talk therapy was helping me, I was never encouraged to share my spiritual philosophies and systems of belief as valid and respected. All my therapists were opposed to religious thinking and so it was not something I could seriously reflect on and grapple with in my sessions. Furthermore, therapy approaches like CBT (cognitive behavioral therapy), for example, are not designed to incorporate social issues as a context for mental illness, but are focused on making people functional enough to keep going in the context of ongoing social harm (which we might be experiencing as racism, sexism, transphobia, white supremacy, climate change, etc.).

A Tarot Therapy practice however can be a vehicle for realizing our radical and liberatory politics. It can speak to the needs of individuals and societies, addressing both the personal and the political. I practice Tarot Therapy for myself in my daily life, and I extend this into community care each week in my wellness community, House of Black. During community readings, we are always reflecting on the world we live in and our responsibility and hope for change.

Tarot Therapy therefore goes beyond the clinical boundaries of talking therapies. It isn't an hour-long safe space of questioning; it is a timeless dialogue with questions with replies and suggestions. It is not detached in the same way talk therapy is; it is invested, involved, and opinionated. It could be a question about a relationship you are pining over and the reply could be the cards The Devil, The Tower, and the Three of Swords. An unequivocal message that this is detrimental to you. You can of course take the conversation further to inquire why you feel so energized to connect to a relationship that is harmful. But a tarot reading is not neutral and withholding, and more specifically when we engage in spirit communication through the cards, there are aspects of consent—a spirit may not agree to discuss particular topics.

Conversations can be refused (as I've experienced often). Sometimes a client will come to me to discuss their finances, and while I always try to make sure their questions are addressed, there is sometimes a detour. I sometimes have to say, "I'm sorry, but the intention of great spirit is to discuss something more pressing: you are here to discuss money but the reading is showing you are chronically depressed and heartbroken and are at the edge of giving up." There have even been times where I have given a gentle and graceful warning that there is a message about abuse; and each time that client has become vulnerable about something they have had to silence and suppress in other parts of their lives. People often think their secrets or the things they are ashamed of will not come up in a reading. But each time, tarot reveals something. It is raw and exposing. You come to a reading to be fully seen (and held without judgment), and that is therapeutic.

Using tarot as a therapy tool also completely informs what kinds of questions we ask, and that in turn shapes the kind of healing experiences that become possible for us. For example, instead of "Will so and so ever come back to me?" we might ask, "I feel very attached to this person, is there something I need to understand about the dynamic or the role of this person in my life?" Perhaps you get an answer that gives you a strategy for release or emotional detachment. For example, you need time away to grieve, or it would help you to let go of their belongings, or maybe travel or start dating again—there are many possibilities. Alternatively, maybe the reading does indicate that you and this person have unfinished business, and how you might manage your life during the interim until you are both in a place to address it. By asking constructive questions that honor your sense of agency, at each step of Tarot Therapy you are able to have a compassionate dialogue that makes your well-being primary, rather than leaving you to the fates and choices of others in your life.

Tarot Therapy, however, isn't about *empowerment*, because that can be a false promise. Sometimes we are facing life circumstances, or feelings that are overpowering us, and we need a space to be honest and frank about that. Sometimes we don't need to wrestle ourselves and others for more power. We need to surrender. Tarot Therapy is about healthy connection. Firstly to ourselves, and then other life-supporting experiences and relationships. It is about true intimacy—restoring the fullness of feeling and our multi-sensory abilities in a life we so often have to shut down from and numb out just to survive.

HOW TO WORK WITH THIS BOOK

You will notice that the chapters of this book deal with the twenty-two major arcana tarot cards only. My approach to Tarot Therapy is to talk about some of the major life issues that we currently face in our different walks of life. Such as our desire to experience **love** (**chapter 1**) and intimacy. Our questions about our life **purpose** (**chapter 2**) and direction. Or our need to escape the grip of working to exhaustion and to experience deep rest and **healing** (**chapter 3**). As well as our internal questions about what we believe and our relationship to **truth** (**chapter 5**), how we can actually use the tarot for **change** (**chapter 4**), and how to build **hope** (**chapter 6**) and resilience by embracing taboo emotions such as anger. These archetypal themes are exactly the kinds of topics addressed through the major arcana and are the necessary foundation to understanding further explorations of the minor arcana in the future.

You do not have to read through this book chronologically. You can choose a chapter by a theme you find particularly interesting or relevant to you at the time. Each chapter has a group of major arcana cards that guide us through the discussion. I do not use the major arcana in chronological order. Instead, the intentional combination of cards (for example The Chariot, The Lovers, and The Star for chapter 3) is part of my meaning-making process, and a real-time demonstration of how you can use the tarot to imagine, contemplate, and find truth in your own life.

When we use a well-shuffled deck, the tarot cards will come up in many different combinations. By discussing the major arcana cards non-chronologically, I am giving a practical example of how we create points of meaning between tarot cards.

Each chapter stands on its own merit as tarot commentary on an important social issue that will be personally relevant to you. This book is intimate and honest because that is what a tarot reading feels like. In my writing I let you into private and vulnerable moments in my life as an example of the meanings of the cards because I believe storytelling—especially the act of listening and being heard—can be a therapeutic process. Without this, *Tarot Therapy* would be a book of detached spiritual analysis. That is not what I wanted to write. Therapy takes time; likewise, this book isn't a quick read with tarot tips to get fast results for a successful life. It is written to be a beautiful traveling therapy area in your mind that you can withdraw to for inner peace.

The chapters are loosely divided into two parts: the beginning of each chapter covers "the journey" where I talk about my personal experience of the issues; and this is then followed by "the healing" where I share the wisdom of the tarot on the topic. There will be times when the ideas in this book feel complex or new to you and that's a normal aspect of spiritual exploration. I have put ◐ in the places where a pause for reflection or slowing down might be helpful. Alongside the exploration of the major arcana cards, you will also come across Tarot Therapy reflection questions that you can use, along with the wisdom in this book, to apply to your own life. If you own a tarot deck, you can pull cards as you come to these questions and begin a Tarot Therapy session for yourself. If you don't have a tarot deck, you can journal about the questions, or bring them up in talk therapy.

Tarot Therapy Reflections

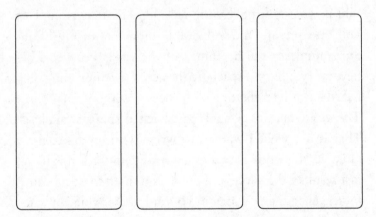

For each Tarot Therapy reflection question, you will be invited to pull three cards. If you are very experienced with tarot readings you can come up with your own spreads for the questions or pull cards in your own style if you would like to. However, the three-card pull is a reliable foundation practice that can be used for readers at all levels. This book explores healing through the themes of the *major arcana,* but when you are pulling cards for the reflection questions you are likely to also get cards from the *minor arcana.* If you need help with the meanings there is a reference guide at the back of this book that gives you simple meanings for the cards to help you interpret your reading.

You can look at the three tarot cards as telling a story about you (beginning, middle, and end). Or you can see the tarot card answers as a passage of time in your life experiences (past, present, future). Alternatively, you can see each of the three cards as three different answers to that question. The practice will resonate differently for different people. What's most important is that you trust yourself enough to give this a try and that you keep an open heart about the answers from the tarot cards. Don't feel intimidated by the example below if you are quite new to reading cards. Focus on the images in the tarot cards you pull and allow them to guide you through possible answers to the questions.

Let's do an example together:

This is a reflection question from chapter 1—*Am I open-hearted and secure or do I tend to be fearful and guarded?* Here's a possible reflective interpretation (beginning, middle, end):

4 of Swords—*Generally you focus on maintaining a peaceful disposition and keeping a neutral attitude about others. You tend toward solitude but are open to connections with others that do not disturb the emotional safety you have created for yourself.*

5 of Cups—*Recently, you have experienced a profound loss, and sadness overshadows you. You have become withdrawn while deeply wanting to be rescued from that state.*

2 of Pentacles—*Your sense of balance and equilibrium is easily thrown off by the thoughts and actions of others. You previously sought to control this by having a lot of alone time. It could be time to find a new way of dealing with this by understanding the cause.*

Here's another possible reflective interpretation (past, present, future):

The Empress—*In the past you were very openhearted and giving. You may have been put on a pedestal by others or found that people became very dependent on you. You were a source of love and nurturing and you enjoyed expressing a maternal instinct toward your loved ones. But you also felt at times that you had to be self-sufficient when it came to your own emotional needs, and didn't have other spiritual equals to depend on.*

Temperance—*Having learned from the past, your focus now is creating reciprocal relationships with others. You understand that you won't always be giving the same amounts, but healthy relationships also require you to receive what others have to offer and to allow them the independence and maturity to show you what they will give. Sometimes you still find things falling out of balance,* *but you know it is an active process of adjusting within changing relationships.*

Wheel of Fortune—*You are very openhearted and trusting. In the future you will have more experiences that teach you the balance of being detached and reserved as you explore life from a different perspective. The main challenge for you ahead is being adaptable to the changes of life and not getting stuck in behavioral comfort zones of always responding in a particular way.*

Here's a final example for if you are very new to tarot that uses a keyword approach:

The Hermit—Keywords: Contemplation, Solitude, Withdrawal. *Yes, you tend to be guarded. You protect yourself by remaining alone emotionally and physically.*

King of Wands—Keywords: Leadership, Charisma, Ambition. *You are strong-minded and don't like to consult others or be instructed on what to do. You are guarded about your independence.*

Knight of Cups—Keywords: Romantic, Seductive, Playful. *You are not emotionally available to others and only overcome your guarded nature to enjoy playful or sensual time with others without attachments or commitments.*

The Tarot Therapy reflection questions in this book are also suitable for answering together with others; in fact, I encourage it. Do the spreads together with trusted friends and peers. Talk about the cards you get; maybe your friends will even be able to recognize how those themes come up in your life and offer you illuminating reflections. Whether you choose to explore this book in the company of others or alone, it is my intention that it creates a safe way for you to develop a healthy practice of the tarot and offers a reflection of life that supports you becoming more free, honest, connected, and loved.

COMMON QUESTIONS
ON TAROT THERAPY

Who are you talking to when you pull cards?

This is a common question I get about tarot. The answer to that has been different over my years of practice. It began as an extension of an inner dialogue, getting clarity about my own thoughts and feelings. As I developed personally and cultivated a spiritual practice, the tarot became more than a psychological profile. It became part of the dialogue I have with the divine and unseen world. The mysticism I had rejected in the beginning became the center of my tarot relationship. I realized I could not reject the future-telling aspect of tarot because it was essential to living with a politically informed theology of hope. I needed the tarot to be part of how I dreamed and created a vision of life beyond the limitations of the present or the pervasive suffering in my life and the world around me. I needed to be able to see far and wide. Restricting the parameters of my tarot use was my way of protecting myself from rejection in a hyper-rational world; one that I was entrenched in through my academic path, that would brand me crazy for using occult tools. Removing that limitation meant my Tarot Therapy practice expanded beyond the limits of my experiences to my being advised, guided, and nurtured by wise and honorable dead who love me.

The cards themselves are just paper with pictures. It is about who you choose to let the cards put you in touch with: your future selves (understanding yourself as timeless and asking wisdom of the version of you already living the reality you want to become present); a particular deity the deck illustration seeks to evoke; or maybe you are dialing in to something specific and close to you, an ancestor, a spirit guide of personal resonance. Tarot can put us in conversation with nature and divinity, and that to me is one of the most therapeutic relationships there is.

How do I heal with Tarot Therapy?

The tarot can blueprint, signal, and call out. It can comfort and encourage. But it is not the process of reading the tarot that does the work itself. Tarot is diagnostic, but it is not healing on its own. It names but it does not change. To use tarot in a therapeutic practice is to make it a guide and signpost in our efforts for recovery. It's what you *do* with what you see that creates change; and this is why community is vital in helping us take the next steps to make the changes we want to.

Can I do Tarot Therapy with any tarot reader?

There are different approaches to tarot reading, and it is helpful to know how and why you use the tarot, as well as the skill or strengths of any tarot readers you go to. For example, not all tarot readers are focused on methods of healing. Or some readers aren't able to discern future events and timelines (that is, possible trajectories along which life events will unfold). My timing specialism is doorways, crossroads, and transitions, so I deal with all directions of time (past, present, and future). But I also have relationships with very skillful readers who deal firmly with the "now" and advise on what is most present. A tarot reader will define for themselves their tarot specialisms, and you should always ask or observe what they say the purpose of their tarot practice is.

For example, for some readers, their practice could be instructional or cautionary rather than therapeutic. Tarot Therapy is defined by the questioning approach used and the goal of maintaining agency while focusing on mental and emotional well-being in daily life. This can be practical and simple, or as advanced and esoteric as healing your ancestral bloodlines. It is up to you and/or the tarot reader to decide the parameters of use and how you would like your practice to grow.

Can Tarot Therapy tell me about my future?

While Tarot Therapy emphasizes the present, sometimes we really do need advice and support about what is coming next. Addressing our fears about the future and choices we need to make can be the best thing we can do to bring peace and balance to our lives. We don't have to be fatalistic or pessimistic in the ways we give attention to the present. We shouldn't use the present to avoid being hopeful. Tarot Therapy can very much be about the future, especially the healed and balanced lives we are seeking to develop.

What kinds of tarot decks are used for Tarot Therapy?

The tarot deck you use matters and can influence the types of conversations and answers it is possible to have. I like to use indie decks and decks that specifically represent Black folk—not just in image but also in culture and philosophy. I have some decks by incredible visionaries that share a perspective for a more just society. I have decks that center on specific deities, and others that are nature based. The philosophy and outlook of a tarot deck matters to the question you are asking. I don't have absolutes, but, for example, if I am asking about finances and career I am unlikely to use an erotic deck that is themed around sex, love, and pleasure. Your ancestors may have deck preferences because the symbols are culturally resonant; this could even be according to religion. I know some people who aren't Christian but their ancestors were, and so they like to use biblical symbolism in communication.

Is Tarot Therapy something I can do alone?

Yes, the questioning and deepening of self-awareness through Tarot Therapy can be practiced alone in quiet reflection. However, healing is not individualistic; it is done in community. The truths that come through Tarot Therapy should lead you into deeper intimacy and connection with others as you find the courage to live in your authenticity. For example, even when we practice tarot solo, it is helpful to share our insights and reflections with friends and loved ones. They can support and affirm our growth process, and they also learn and develop by observing our courage to change.

1

LOVE

WHERE TO GO WHEN IN SEARCH OF LOVE
The High Priestess, The Empress, The Emperor

Everything in life is better when we feel loved. Our days are in full technicolor with the sound turned up. Love is driving alone through the idyllic greenery of the English countryside on a rare gloriously hot British weekend. It's the beauty of black clamshells clinging to the rocks of Portugal's beaches. Or witnessing the warmth of the local community from the heights of Brazil's Sugarloaf Mountain. It's a home-cooked meal. It's new places and experiences. It's the kindness of animal companions and the delighted chuckle of infants. Love in all its forms makes us feel *alive*.

Which is peculiar, because blood, oxygen, and flesh are the things life is made of. Doctors don't administer love to dying patients in hospitals; love is not a vital sign of life. In Western patriarchal capitalist culture, love is only valued as an appetite. Something we crave and are compelled by. It's a desire we would (and, in many cases, do) spend and spend and spend on to satisfy. Images of love are prevalent all throughout our popular culture—in our art and global media—and at the same time, love as a subject is critically missing in so many crucial places. It's not a topic in our national politics, nor are we taught how to love in school; it is rarely given serious thought and inquiry. Even when we explore mental health we may mention *care*, but not necessarily love. It is quite the trick that love is everywhere; whether it's present or absent, it is something we are always negotiating and responding to, trying to find balance in a minefield of personal relationships. Yet it is paradoxically trivialized. In our failure to have a broad cultural conversation about love as significant to the experience and meaning of life, it is represented as something elusive and ephemeral, a bonus, a personal luxury, the luck of the draw. Not something we can create and actively work toward, but something we can only hope to encounter by chance.

WHY DOES LOVE MATTER?

Love is an experience we are longing to understand. It is the most popular question of all the tarot readings I have done over the years, because it speaks to our *quality* of life. We can exist, work, and pass the days. But what I've become sure of is we cannot bear life without love. We cannot be aware of ourselves and connected to the body, feeling everything from euphoria to devastation. We cannot live through the range of experiences of one hundred years or less on Earth, with our sense of well-being whole and intact, without loving and being loved. Love experienced in its myriad aspects will always be the only truly compelling reason to keep going.

Part of the difficulty of recognizing love's presence is that it isn't tangible. Or something we can go out and get when we want it. It has to be slowly and consistently nurtured and developed, or even conjured and drawn into existence in the alchemical blends of our different lives, actions, and experiences. Love can be unpredictable and arbitrary. Even ineffable—that is, beyond our ability to put into words. How many times have you been asked why you love someone, and in response stumbled your way through a list of some of their better qualities? It isn't definitive. *Love is an elevation.* You don't respond in the same way to everyone who is confident, or funny, or beautiful. Those things, though appealing, are not love itself. We can differentiate between love as *affect* (the way we are moved by emotion), and our acts of service to each other (love as action and commitment). But in the end, its mystery persists, so that we are much better at saying what love is *not*; of speaking to how it feels to be unloved, or the grief and despair of losing love, or the pining and emptiness of seeking love and not finding it.

In my early twenties I read *All About Love: New Visions* by Black feminist writer bell hooks, and I knew, in dialogue with her, that I had found my life's work. This book is part of a trilogy in which hooks invites us into the intimacy of the missing conversation about love in popular culture. She explores our polarized society and asks the question "What Is Love?" to guide us toward healing and new paths to experiencing truly satiating and spiritually expansive love. I felt relieved that hooks had demonstrated to me that love was a worthwhile subject of study, because understanding love had long been an informal passion project of mine. Following her legacy as one of the most important Black women scholars and activists of our time, similarly I have always written, thought, and spoken about love and its absence. I wasn't just preoccupied with love because I'd played with Barbies as a child, watched Disney films right into my adulthood, or enjoyed the glamor of romantic Hollywood films as much as the next person. I don't deny that all this conditioned me to have certain expectations for my life, but I was being stirred into interest by something else.

It's the reason, raised in a religious home, the Gospel of John with his declaration "God is love" was my favorite. Or why the films *Blue Valentine* and *The Lobster* were my instant classics, winning me over with their dystopian cynicism about the possibilities of romantic love. Before Zooey Deschanel charmed us in the hit TV comedy *New Girl*, I knew her as the antihero of the film *500 Days of Summer*, with that infamous "expectations versus reality" scene. (If you haven't seen this iconic moment, it's where there are two parallel scenes on screen with different outcomes. One side shows the main character's expectation of having a wonderfully romantic evening at a party with his love interest, where they are wrapped up in their feelings for each other. On the other side of the screen, you see the reality of how things played out, where she is disinterested and dismissive and he spends the party alone and awkward, only to find out she has just become engaged!)

I was interested in love because it was not ubiquitous in the way the artists of our time seemed to promise. This was my very own expectation-versus-reality moment in life. The dream of romantic love did not even begin to cover the disconnect between what I'd imagined about love and what I was experiencing: the lack of it.

LOVELESSNESS

As a young Black woman, throughout my adulthood the promise of intimacy and care seemed to be evading me despite my best efforts. There were many ways I and others around me were experiencing what bell hooks described in her work as a state of "lovelessness." This was the first time I found that my confusion and mistakes and sense of loneliness were so powerfully spoken to in a book. When she discussed the tense relationships in her family as a social and cultural issue, I saw my own estrangement from my parents as part of that context. For the first time I understood that it wasn't a personal failing on my part. I wasn't too flawed or unlovable. What was happening to me, the lack of love, was a widespread cultural phenomenon, an estrangement having an effect on everyone. This was not new (though there are specific ways my identity and relationship to power in society have defined the availability and possibility of love for me, as is the case for each of us). But as with our parents, and their parents before them, it is my generation's turn to grapple with feeling starved of love. Our turn to decide what love could mean for us, and what our possibilities are for ful-filling our spiritual and emotional needs.

This is a question that should be asked and answered by each of us, and so this chapter is not advice for unhappy people that the contented should generally skip. You could be in blissful love right now, or full of gratitude for a supportive family or friendship group, but love is not a meal we consume only once; it is a hunger we satiate over a lifetime. There is never too much love. The more there is, and the fuller we feel, the more we are inspired to give. If you are soaking and basking in the sweetness of love, then you are also the subject of this chapter, because in a love drought your exquisite joy is vital to life. It is just as important that you learn to protect and sustain it.

Many of us do not even recognize that we are experiencing lovelessness. As hooks writes in *All About Love*, "living with lovelessness is not a problem we openly and readily complain about." But it can show up as chronic self-reliance and individualism—believing we have to do everything for ourselves and experiencing shame and fear when faced with asking for help. Lovelessness can be wanting to experience intimacy and share our life journey with others but finding companionship lacking or confined within the boundaries of friendship. Though being a space for profoundly loving experiences, the bonds of friendship can still leave other aspects of our need for love untouched. It's like having a delicious gourmet meal but still being thirsty. Hunger and thirst are different needs, and one kind of love does not necessarily compensate for all the other ways we want to grow, mature, and experience ourselves through love.

We can miss that we are struggling with lovelessness by bingeing on entertainment as a substitute for the nourishment of love. Renewing our sources of temporary happiness as often as possible in the feeling of having or buying something new. At its most destructive, lovelessness is the burden and struggle of daily survival; living with stress and insecurity, fearing over physical safety. The crisis of financial instability can keep us in a perpetual fight that makes love an afterthought or distraction. Something we feel we can only engage in when we are finally safe. Or worse, lead us to chasing love in an addictive way to avoid life circumstances that are continually worsening.

THE SEARCH FOR LOVE

When lovelessness continues to impact us without intervention, its effects on us go beyond the scope of what happiness can keep at bay. I was overwhelmingly happy when I graduated from university, first class with honors, and I went on to successfully apply for a scholarship to do my master's, which had been my dream—it was an undisputed high point in my life. However, within weeks I couldn't get out of bed or shower or eat, and eventually I couldn't go in to the new job I had been headhunted for. I had so many great things happening in my life, but what was fueling my descent? I had been single-minded

TAROT THERAPY REFLECTION

Shuffle and pull three tarot cards, or journal
and discuss with a therapist or friends:
"IN WHAT AREAS OF LIFE MIGHT I
BE AVOIDING OR STRUGGLING WITH
FEELINGS OF LOVELESSNESS?"

_____

_____

_____

_____

_____

_____

_____

_____

_____

_____

_____

about attaining my educational goals, and there I was in the wake of achievement finally left with the space to feel the things I had pushed downward: I didn't feel loved. I was in fact loved by many people around me, and I knew it, but I felt numb and disconnected. I was locked out of myself with no safe way in. What you couldn't see in my graduation photos, or the beautiful background of Westminster City in my lunch-break social media posts, is that I was experiencing severe trauma as a result of lovelessness. I had been excelling by social standards, and so no one really understood what was happening—not even me—until I just couldn't go on anymore.

Recent mental health advocacy has brought talk therapy into the mainstream as a healthy response to everyday life challenges, but before this it was uncommon for people to discuss personal life difficulties as being traumatizing. Trauma isn't just the big, bone-breaking things in life— war, car accidents, and so on. Trauma unfolds through shock and disruption, and often when we are met with the force of a person or experience that removes our sense of personal power and agency over ourselves. It is one of the main ways we get stuck in feelings of lovelessness.

We can experience chronic trauma over a long period of time when we can't leave a disempowering environment, like a highly stressful job or an unhappy home. Or there is complex trauma when we have repeated incidents of exposure to something that causes us severe emotional pain. After consecutive relationship breakdowns our trauma can show up in the recurring thought, *People always leave me,* for example.

Our deficit of love is all the ways we end up isolated from individual and communal nurturing and sanctuary. In 2020, when many of us experienced a global pandemic for the first time, and distance and isolation were mandatory, we became hyperaware of our need for close bonds with others—as well as the points of discomfort involved with one of the staples of talk therapies: sitting with oneself. Stillness gathers everything to the surface. With the noise and excitement of the outside world being boarded up and closed off, we were forced into a quiet place, not necessarily having the skills to process all the thoughts, emotions, and memories we were suddenly left with. Not to mention essential workers who were experiencing a different kind of isolation by having to continue—with fear, exhaustion, uncertainty, and even grief—when so much else in the world had stopped. It recalls the change and isolation I referred to after graduating and leaving the large social community university provides, being at a distance from friends I had lived with and seen every day for years, and losing the daily structure of lectures and classes. My systems of support were suddenly gone.

Being separated from the things and people we love (which was the overwhelming feeling of the pandemic but definitely not specific only to that time), and losing the stability of positive life experiences (if we can say we were having many of them to begin with), made the loveless conditions of our culture plain and obvious. People were finding new ways to create meaning or to grapple with long-term feelings of disconnection. In a time of mass death and thinking about a possible future, the choice to

TAROT THERAPY REFLECTION

Shuffle and pull three tarot cards, or journal
and discuss with a therapist or friends:
"WHERE IN MY LIFE, OR WITH WHOM,
ARE THERE TRUE EXPERIENCES OF THE
LOVE I CURRENTLY NEED?"

_____

_____

_____

_____

_____

_____

_____

_____

_____

_____

_____

live a life filled with love in all its iterations was more pertinent than ever. The question posed to all of us is, where do you go in search of love?

The High Priestess

Initiation, intuition, higher realms,
mystery, spirituality, inner voice,
secrets, wisdom, magic,
alternate knowledge, occult, hidden

We can recognize The High Priestess as the seer, the conjuror, the hoodoo and the root worker; the diviner, the oracle, and the medicine woman. She can be the parent who tells you not to go out tonight because they had a dream. Or the grandmother who bathes with herbs cut from the garden and throws water over the threshold of the front door every morning. She's in all the divination arts carefully revealing the secrets of the heart. And of course, she is right there in the tarot cards. Major arcana number two.

We encounter The High Priestess as the paradoxically well-adjusted person; when so many others are uncertain and disconnected, she seems to have a secret source of faith and trust that keeps her full. She is someone whose peace or mirth is a contradiction when her challenging life circumstances are accounted for, because like everyone else she has made mistakes and suffered. We feel drawn to or inspired by the energy of The High Priestess because of her wisdom and vitality: her life force is strong. She knows something we obviously do not, and in a love drought when we grow tired of temporary comforts, we look for someone to show us how to feel connected to ourselves.

As an experienced tarot practitioner and friend, I have been a High Priestess to many. As societies destabilize politically and culturally, and people return to contending with the uncertain and unknown, there has been a resurgence of interest in the divination arts. Admittedly, most new patrons of tarot readings are looking for another way to feel secure about their future again. They may ask, "Will I get this job?" or "Will I find a romantic partner?"

For those of us who have an intimate knowledge of the sacred role of The High Priestess, we know that people who put their trust in us need more than a promise of future fortune in the form of love or money. Through the tarot we are able to explore with others the possibilities of living and creating through mystery. Teaching them the ways to connect with their inner High Priestess to discern where they are on their path. Whether they are near or far from their goals and desires, sabotaging themselves or being disrupted by others, or creating possibilities with the resources around them. We show them how to stand, like the illustrations of The High Priestess tarot card, between fixed pillars of knowledge and continuously draw through and add to the structures of life their unique perspectives and otherworldly inspirations.

The otherworldliness is emphasized because that is the secret The High Priestess welcomes us into. She stands comfortably in the darkness because she cultivates her knowledge from a secret internal place. The symbolism of The High Priestess is associated with the moon as a planetary body, and with the zodiac sign Pisces as some-one working with ether (the vastness of time-space) and the state before conception (all creative possibilities; what could come into being as a result of our choices). For this reason, The High Priestess is the perfect place to go when we are feeling stuck. Or when our actions seem to keep yielding the same results, or when we do not know where or how to begin.

When we need The High Priestess, she could show up as someone who reminds you that you are the best au-thority on discovering the answers to who you are and what you need. You may have experienced a coup; a par-ent, an overbearing friend, even the state attempting to define this for you. Even if you have lost your autonomy and your ability to trust yourself, in The High Priestess you can find a process of retrieval that gradually puts you back in the front seat.

When we encounter the presence of The High Priest-ess in a tarot reading it's a reminder to work with alter-native systems of knowledge, and to emphasize personal wisdom over external validation and social convention. Her confronting gaze asks us to admit when we are wres-tling against an inner truth because there is something external—logic, tradition, our past experiences, physical restrictions and so on—that says we are wrong or at least being naive. She asks you to become conscious of your intuitive thoughts and feelings that may have become ob-scured without having to present them as proof to others. You have nothing to prove. What is a truth that is only known to you?

The High Priestess ultimately initiates us into the work of self-inquiry. This is a crucial intervention because the realization of love—of all kinds—does not have a fixed set of rules. Doing what your parents did, or what your friends advise, or following the steps of someone else's journey may not give the results you want or need. This isn't a rejection of the insights and care of others; we *need* this. Our actions will impact the people around us, and who we are or can become unfolds in the matrix of our relationships. But we squander the gift, majesty, and the potential blooming of a budding life when we fail to mature and embrace our individuality.

The multiple routes and doorways to more love and connection in our lives can only be opened through the map of our intuition and internal truths. The journey can be shared, but the directions are only for you. When we walk in our truth, we find the company of others traveling in the same direction. Sometimes we call these people soulmates, because their extraordinary kindredness is life-affirming. The beauty and joy in connecting says we are seen and celebrated for the choices we've made to arrive at this point and to share ourselves. In the companionship of others, we have a home we can travel with. How could we ever feel lost again?

But before we take residence in the hearts of others, the nudge of The High Priestess is a reminder that the journey is a moving thing. We don't know how we'll be impacted by changes in direction as we grow. How long our paths can twist and wind and weave around the other like vines without distorting into an obstructive weed. We don't know whether all parties are willing and have the tools to grow so closely together. It is a constant balancing act of navigating and rebalancing personal boundaries.

It is not uncommon to hear casual talk about boundaries or to have a disagreement where it is pointed out "This is not my stuff" (a callout for emotional baggage claim, because therapeutic language has dispersed into the mainstream). If we've been exploring wellness and healing topics then we are alert to habits of codependency, enmeshment, and overextension; this means to feel we are unable to function independent of a relationship, or our boundaries are so permeable that we cannot tell apart our own emotions from the other person's. We may have become aware of times when we have not advocated for ourselves and unwittingly been victimized by responding to draining emotional connections in the form of the demands of others. It is part of our maturation to reshape relationships as we learn more about what is healthy for us, and it leaves room for us to be independent.

Up until now we have discussed the boundaries we hold with others, but where it concerns our inner lives The High Priestess exemplifies a different type of boundary: not walls, but doorways. Choosing what kinds of ideas, beings, and experiences we want to cross paths with. The same work to become self-aware can grant an enjoyable connection with all that is. She initiates us into the use of plant medicines, somatic movement, massage therapy and other kinds of bodywork, meditation, yoga, ancestral connection and ritual, spiritual cleansing practices, voice and breathwork, visualization, and so much more, as an answer to the love drought in our hearts. She also invites us into communion with kind and wise ancestors, deities, angels, and animal spirit guides. Her answer—standing at the nexus of creation—is that there is always more for you to experience than you think the present moment holds. At the crossroads of our lives she introduces us to two allies as forces of change: The Empress and Emperor.

The Empress

Fertility, nurturing, creativity,
cycles and rhythms, motherhood,
femininity, beauty, abundance,
resourcefulness, attraction, receptivity

The Empress is associated with creativity, fertility, beauty, and motherhood. Traditionally pictured sitting in a lush grove, she represents our capacity to take what we are given and to multiply it into even greater possibilities for expression. As a symbol of the womb or creatrix (a female creator), The Empress teaches that even in scarcity we can create more if we use what we have—no matter how little or limited. Either because we build on it, multiplying it as we go along, or because we metaphorically eat it (use it up) to sustain us on the path to conditions that are more suitable for love to grow. Love, in this context, refers to everything that satiates the soul.

The Empress is magnetic and attractive, and her main functions are openheartedness and the cultivation of what she is offered from others. This, however, can lead to the "poisoning of the well" if the seed she blooms is violence, bitterness, or pain. So, The Empress is necessarily self-protective, evolving walls and barriers against the imposing force of others that risk transforming her into the mother of death (who is a separate and well-loved deity in her own right). If her generous boundaries are violated, The Empress is capable of being closed-off and self-sustaining—denying others her beauty and grace. The Empress of the tarot is likely an iteration of the Greek goddess Demeter (goddess of agriculture, harvest, and fertility), who refused to let anything grow when her daughter Persephone was stolen by Hades, god of the underworld. Therefore, The Empress also represents the refusal to create without the right conditions. Without safety and trust, the abundant scene of The Empress card can quickly decline into destruction and death.

Through The Empress we recognize the challenge to remain open and receptive in our lives when there are many different ways to come into contact with pain. Worse, for pain, fear, shame, or melancholy to grow within like a wildfire that burns away our innocence, leaving us raw and shut down. This is ultimately how we end up in the emotional and social wasteland that is lovelessness. Embodying the injured Empress who is inherently creative, we can reproduce our pain in our relationships with each other.

TAROT THERAPY REFLECTION

Shuffle and pull three tarot cards, or journal
and discuss with a therapist or friends:
"AM I OPENHEARTED AND SECURE,
OR DO I TEND TO BE FEARFUL AND
GUARDED?"

_____

_____

_____

_____

_____

_____

_____

_____

_____

_____

_____

Our worthiness to experience love is not determined by an external value system or whether we think others recognize us as deserving and lovable. It is derived from being able to give ourselves to the world from a place of deep self-trust in the inner High Priestess. That's what we lose when we shut ourselves down. We tend to judge that we have betrayed ourselves, behaved foolishly, trusted our hearts when we shouldn't have. We may feel we were overpowered and compelled by our emotions to do things we otherwise would not. When we wrestle back control over ourselves, we feel we can't risk being taken to that place again. Of everything we lose contact with when we close ourselves off, it's the silencing of The High Priestess—voice of our intuition—that is most detrimental.

Maybe it's true that we have said and done things that have been a betrayal of ourselves or of others, but does that mean we should reject ourselves and deny the beauty, wisdom, and truth that we are capable of? The Empress as maternal symbol reminds us that our mistakes are also part of our love story. Not just as lessons we gain about how to do better, but as moments of *receiving* love when we need it most. When we have messed up, failed, or feel we have made a fool of ourselves, can we let down our guard enough to offer ourselves compassion and forgiveness? Or to learn from the common inner conflict of heart versus mind? Can we offer ourselves patience with the process, or do we abandon ourselves in criticism and self-punishment? Can we gain information that deepens self-trust, repairs the walls of our boundaries, and increases our awareness of personal red flags? The internal Empress is the maternal instinct we develop toward ourselves because even as adults we will always require mothering, and of all the acts of love, being gentle with ourselves can be the hardest one.

LOVE IS COMMUNAL

The logic of self-love is that the beginning of love is always nurtured within. While this is true, there is no purpose for being open and receptive if love is only to be cultivated alone. We cannot single-handedly grow a personal garden that is only sustainable through a wide variety of loving experiences; this has to come about through relational exchange with others.

By understanding the creation and experience of love as a shared practice we ensure its longevity. We are able to divide the responsibility for reciprocating love (which strengthens and multiplies it) so that a loss, or even a series of traumas, does not disrupt those pathways, leaving us disconnected. Instead, like a child loved by a large family, we have many routes and places we can go to when we have suffered a loss in one.

Self-love is our location and center in a sprawling grid of communal love that also serves as a boundary against others who mean us harm. When we belong to communities of love, we are strengthened to set genuine boundaries with others because we are not love-starved. Therefore, we don't have to compromise our values to feed the parts of ourselves we need to survive (intimacy, connection,

TAROT THERAPY REFLECTION

Shuffle and pull three tarot cards, or journal
and discuss with a therapist or friends:
"WHAT DO I NEED FORGIVENESS OR
COMPASSION FOR?"

_____

_____

_____

_____

_____

_____

_____

_____

_____

_____

_____

_____

validation). For example, there were times in my life that I endured unwanted experiences in exchange for that one thing I needed. Times that I had sex with someone, when I only wanted to be held or listened to; this was an unspoken negotiation for having my emotional needs met that I otherwise felt I could not ask for, or would not be granted.

We therefore do not love alone. When we are loved in a sustainable way it involves both protection and intimacy. It ensures that we can be open and receptive with a sense of safety and trust and that others willingly share their pleasures and their love, and will create space for us. In this dwelling we have cause and inspiration to create and to grow for generations to come. Even when there is pain or harm we don't wither and give up internally, but we are watered and healed by the lakes of love around us. Places we are welcome to because we have also been tending to them over time. If we were to rely on self-love alone, any love drought would eventually lead us right back to inner feelings of lovelessness.

The Empress, seated confidently on her throne, embodies the lesson to enjoy love within a community of people and to feel worthy of being the center. This isn't because the world revolves around us, but because in the grid of loving connections we can only see from the orientation of where we are positioned. Moreover, our points of connection only light up when they meet the ignition of our own love. If we cannot generate it, there can be love circulating to us that we can't participate in; like a single blown light bulb in a string of many.

One of the ways we learn self-love is by replicating the love we extend to others. Love is the ultimate mirror revealing us to ourselves through the eyes and actions of another. It allows us to become more than we already are. There are versions of ourselves that we require no convincing to like when there is love present as the casting director in the story of our lives. Love is like a sun that signals us to grow like a plant, to extend branches of ourselves that otherwise would have no cause to come into being: this is how we discover ourselves as The Emperor.

The Emperor

Protection, vision, stability,
masculinity, self-control, autonomy,
authority, discipline, power, leadership,
innovation, success, strength

Associated with the zodiac sign Aries, **The Emperor is an innovator. At every juncture, The Emperor is breaking the wheel and remaking it, in contrast to patriarchal masculinity, under the tutelage of love. This is not an activity that is restricted to men; this is how all of us come to terms with our place in the world and our relationship to power.** Our empire consists of our creations and our field of influence over other people, places, and things. As a co-ruler of the life The Empress has created, each of us as The Emperor has to decide on a long-term vision for ourselves—that is, what kind of impact we want to have and the legacy we want to leave behind. As well as what kinds of power we have access to and how we will choose to use it in aid of ourselves and others. When we choose to act as The Emperor we are deciding on an overall direction, and we adopt responsibility for others who follow in our footsteps. For example, our children, colleagues, or large public communities that we have influence on.

Though The Emperor is commonly considered the intimate counterpart to The Empress, when we decenter a romantic reading of these two cards, The Empress is a mother of The Emperor; she creates him as an expression of herself. It's similar, for example, to making a piece of art and then having to market it or defend it against criticism. It is the development or completion of the creative process. The Empress is the artist, The Emperor follows as the advocate. He is a symbol of power and authority, leadership over others, and commitment to a vision.

It is difficult for our imagination of The Emperor not to be entangled with and distorted by the dominant masculine archetypes that exist under patriarchy as dictator, aggressor, or seducer. But in my close reading of this card in my Tarot Therapy practice, The Emperor is not a representative of men in the world. He is an expression in each of us as a collaborative creation of The High Priestess and The Empress—*a product of love and intuition*. He is the recognition of the need for a defender and protector for true love and safety to be possible.

The Emperor defends the boundaries of our ultimate creation: ourselves. He is our representative, the identity we actively display to the world. As The Empress, we are engaged in the creative process of our learning and

TAROT THERAPY REFLECTION

Shuffle and pull three tarot cards, or journal
and discuss with a therapist or friends:
"WHAT OR WHO DO I NEED TO
PROTECT?"

_____

_____

_____

_____

_____

_____

_____

_____

_____

_____

_____

_____

personal transformation. When we have also found our inner Emperor, his role is to validate and project a strong sense of self. While The Empress is primarily concerned with the nonmaterial aspects of life (thoughts, emotions, etc.), The Emperor finds ways to express this in the outer physical world through art, culture, philosophy, and commerce, etc. The Emperor is concerned with action; he represents the things we do with our lives.

Exploration and challenge are motivators for The Emperor. When it comes to love, he will not choose to stay in places where it is lacking. He is the risk taker and the seeker. He will leave a relationship if it suits him, or start a new business if it feeds his passions. As the creation of The Empress he is familiar with what is beautiful, nurturing, and loving. He does not begin from a place of scarcity, and so he is fearless. The Emperor represents the many cycles of rebirthing ourselves. Each time we learn a life lesson, or encounter a point of wisdom in the outer world, we allow ourselves to be altered. The Emperor is the expression of that confidence. Of our knowing. The High Priestess and The Empress deal with sense, intuition, and impression, but The Emperor has the added benefit of truth and conviction because what he can rationalize and communicate has already passed through the tests of emotion and intuition.

The Emperor is the second draft of your essay or your third driving test: he is experience. Through him we enact our autonomy, self-control, and discipline. We explore the versions of love that come from healthy independence. Being deeply connected to the various parts of the inner self, he is not love-starved, but full of the creativity and passion of The Empress. Because of this, The Emperor is willing to be together *or* alone. Experiencing love in all states. We might notice The Emperor in life as the athlete or solo artist. The entrepreneur or wise and committed family member. The social advocate and humanitarian with a great capacity to care for others. We see The Emperor whenever we meet a visionary or a maverick. Or when we hear someone take the risk to speak truthfully.

The Emperor is a powerful advocate for our inner truths. When we need to connect with our inner Emperor he is activated in response to the challenges of life. Firstly, when we need to protect ourselves; The Emperor is who we become when we choose to fight for our safety, defend our reputation, or protect things that are sacred to us. We are embodying The Emperor when we demand or seek more for ourselves, when we choose to push beyond the limitations of our circumstances with the faith that there could be more. When we affirm that love and abundance aren't fleeting but are crucial to our well-being, we are showing up as The Emperor. Through the self-worth of The Emperor we see that if we experience lovelessness it is not a reason to blame or malign ourselves, but a sign that a system, place, or person is sickly, harmed, or not functioning well, and change is needed. We act as The Emperor when we adopt a strong outward voice for the High Priestess's quiet inner knowing: when we stand in our truth. He represents our implicit trust in ourselves and our willingness to live boldly, to express who we are without shame or apology. Without having the inner strength and confidence of The Emperor, we might not allow ourselves to be known well enough to be loved.

The High Priestess teaches us to hear ourselves and discover our unique abilities. The Empress guides us in being open and vulnerable enough to receive love and express our creativity. The Emperor leads us in the highest path of love, which is to share the fullness of ourselves, to give.

2

PURPOSE

Choosing Your Spiritual Journey

The Moon, The World, The Wheel of Fortune

To go on a personal spiritual journey is to engage in a process of introspection. To find meaning in our life circumstances. To gain knowledge about who we are and the nature of the world around us—particularly, our own role and story within it. This is often a metaphorical journey taken through our minds as we explore ideas that challenge our existing sense of truth or reality. However, a personal spiritual journey can also include physical pilgrimages where we seek out environments that are most conducive to spiritual reflection; traditionally this would be an escape into nature. For example, climbing the peak of a mountain or hill; wandering quietly through forests, by rivers, seas, and lakes; or traversing the harsh and hot conditions of a dune.

Whether physical or mental, the start of every spiritual journey is through symbolic darkness: into the unknown. It is why taking periods of solitude is a major theme of spiritual teachings across all cultures. This does not mean that family, creativity, work, and adventure are less meaningful things to push aside for a "higher spiritual purpose." They require our attention and devotion too. They can, however, become willful distractions from the subtleties of a spiritually led life. Where we can feel pulled in different directions between the more esoteric quiet exploration of the unknown (sometimes seen as a privilege of having the time) and the need to be present and committed to busy and demanding life responsibilities already unfolding around us.

When we take time away for contemplation, our environment transforms into a stimulating backdrop for introspection. Out in nature, for example, as we run, climb, or ascend, we might think about our capacity for patience and endurance in our everyday lives. In the solitude we may notice the lingering inner voice of our doubts and fears. Considering how often similar anxious thoughts are disrupting our day-to-day goals. We may be stirred into hope or reverence by the beauty of a landscape or the bustling of local animal inhabitants. Even if this takes place in a local park or on a morning jog down an urban street, creating space for our peace helps to reintegrate the many parts of ourselves that we separate into the different roles we play—creator, lover, friend, parent, adviser, and so on. It gives us the opportunity to center ourselves as the main characters and to piece together the plot twists and signs in our story as we narrate our lives through thought.

The parallels between the spiritual journey and traveling through nature are the theme of the bestselling novel *The*

TAROT THERAPY REFLECTION

Shuffle and pull three tarot cards, or journal
and discuss with a therapist or friends:
"DO I PRIORITIZE MYSELF AS THE MAIN
CHARACTER IN MY LIFE STORY?"

_____

_____

_____

_____

_____

_____

_____

_____

_____

_____

_____

_____

Alchemist by Paulo Coelho—a book about a young boy's journey of personal discovery that is often recommended to people newly contemplating their spirituality. It was a book that I read several years after a loss of faith and a difficult separation from the religious community that had defined my early life. I had grown up in a strict religious single-parent household where my mother and grandmother were major spiritual influences on me. When my mum—former free-spirited party girl—converted to Christianity, I, as a young child, embarked on a spiritual path with her that preexisted my own personal choices about faith and belief.

Much further down that road, as I was coming into my own as an adult with many unanswered questions and about to leave for university, the sense of meaning and purpose I found in Black activism put me at odds with the church community I had grown up in. To them, my independence, my passion for my culture, and my political engagement threatened the universalism of their teachings that we are all the same under God.

I started a new spiritual journey. One where I wanted to contemplate "God" or the meaning of life in different terms. Where my spirituality could hold room for politics and culture and love—for the fullness of my character. In its simplicity, *The Alchemist* helped to give me the confidence to overcome my fear of the unknown ahead of me. To see that the answers I needed weren't solely in books and classic religious texts. I could find answers to some of my deepest questions through being open to the quest of life unfolding in front of me. Through *my* story.

As I ventured beyond the religious social life I had always known, I met peers and made friends with people who had very different upbringings from mine. They had none of the doubt and pain of the religious trauma I had experienced from being ostracized. When they had come to points in their lives where they were seeking deeper meaning, they found answers in astrology and tarot. These were their tools of introspection and wonder. Together we would sit and look at our astrological birth charts, discovering so much more than the pop zodiac sign advice in magazines that I had always assumed astrology to be. There were methods for understanding my career path, my greatest challenges in love, my vices and shortcomings in my personality, and what kinds of places would be good for me to live in or travel to. As a separate but complementary practice, the tarot animated those lessons through characters, archetypes, and stories. When I pulled the Queen of Pentacles I would see myself as practical and industrious. Or if the 7 of Wands came up, then I would know I was at a stage of life where I would have to apply a lot of effort and stand my ground. Through these stories I started to observe the wisdom in the patterns. Life was showing me something. Weaving and guiding me toward a specific plan.

The Moon

The unknown, secrecy,
illusion, fear, attraction,
sign, subconscious, emotion

The Moon card in the tarot is a symbol for the often invisible nonmaterial parts of life. It is illustrated as two wolves howling at a moon. A path between two towers is illuminated and a crustacean crawls up from the sea onto the land at the beginning of the path. The Moon represents what is concealed—what happens in the depths of the self behind rationality and consciousness and what comes up from below. It deals with things that operate below the surface (subconscious) and the influences that can be present yet unseen and unknown to us unless we investigate them (unconscious). For example, impulses or unconscious beliefs that dictate our behavior. Or, beyond the self, an active environment of spirit characters around us that we are completely unaware of.

People contemporarily use these words that we associate with The Moon card—*subconscious* and *unconscious*—interchangeably to mean the same thing. This is the far-reaching influence of the famous psychoanalyst Sigmund Freud, who wrote about the repressed and inaccessible aspects of a fragmented or disturbed mind. In school we learn that our brains process information from our environment without our active awareness, and these stored memories can affect our choices and actions—this is the

TAROT THERAPY REFLECTION

Shuffle and pull three tarot cards, or journal
and discuss with a therapist or friends:
"ARE THERE PARTS OF MY PERSONALITY
THAT CONCERN ME OR MAKE ME FEEL
OUT OF CONTROL?"

_____

_____

_____

_____

_____

_____

_____

_____

_____

_____

_____

_____

subconscious. Freud introduced the idea of the unconscious as a part of the mind that is inaccessible to us. A place where we repress our thoughts and emotions. It is like the dangerous shadow side of a well-functioning logical mind, that is irrational and out of our control. In this way, the things "below the surface," parts of ourselves that we can't physically see, became characterized in popular media as threatening. The horror genre is a perfect example of this. In Tarot Therapy, however, I work with an understanding of the subconscious and unconscious that are different from these theories by Freud.

THE SUBCONSCIOUS

Through popular Western psychology many of us were only familiar with the subconscious as a place where repressed thoughts and memories go, particularly after a traumatic event. But, in my experience, the subconscious is so much more than that. It is like a quiet inner companion that is always with us, witnessing the events of our lives. It takes in all our sensory experiences (what we see, hear, smell, touch, and taste), using them as information about how to avoid pain and discomfort and instead make choices that lead to more pleasure and self-awareness. It is where our will, desire, and attachments live. In our subconscious we develop patterns, habits, and appetites. It is not fixed and unchangeable; as a part of us it adapts, learns, and grows.

As a constant observer, the subconscious is one of the

best narrators for our personal story. It has stored all our experiences and it knows us well. Unfortunately, because of its unfamiliarity, we have been taught to approach the subconscious with distrust. To attempt to subdue and overcome it through positive thinking and other mindset hacks. So many of us go on for years without the wisdom of the story it has to tell us, and this well-kept story is the key to choosing our spiritual paths.

The crustacean on The Moon card that leaves the sea for the land represents us connecting our subconscious selves with our everyday conscious awareness. The path between two towers on the card is symbolic of beginning to recognize the agency we have in our lives and the power of our choices. We are not just victims of the cycles of life. We don't have to take the routes and do the things that have been long established (tower). We don't have to act on our subconscious urges (wolf) with no way of accounting for our actions because we don't understand how we are being influenced. Rather, through introspection we begin to elevate our subconscious and connect the nonphysical inner aspects ourselves with the tangible outer parts of our day-to-day lives—which is one of the most important *processes*: the "how-to" of developing a spiritual path.

Our subconscious doesn't communicate through words like the conscious mind. Dreams, for example (symbolized by The Moon), are one of the languages used by our subconscious. Many people, however, have no dream recall or discard the subconscious wisdom in their dreams as just white noise or trivial fantasy. We are not very practiced at listening to our subconscious. So, when we do want to connect, we have to find other tools for accessing it. This is what we refer to in spiritual communities as doing "shadow work."

It is said that humans only use 10 percent of our brains, but that doesn't mean the other 90 percent is sinister. Likewise, shadow work is not about exposing and wrangling the monstrous irrational parts of our subconscious selves locked beneath the surface of the rational mind. That is, the parts of ourselves we dislike or have rejected. Rather, shadow work is acknowledging and lovingly integrating the fullness of who we are and our greater capabilities: our spiritual selves, our entire story. Like the two wolves pictured on either side of the path howling at the moon, the subconscious is sending us signs and symbols. The Moon worship of the wolves is a metaphor for honoring our Moon aspects—our intuition, subconscious, and emotions—as methods for finding our way through the uncertainty of a spiritual journey.

Shadow work is therefore an act of self-inquiry. Its aim is to locate resistance and disharmony caused by conflict and miscommunication between the conscious and subconscious parts of ourselves. It can be subtle, like the creaks of an old house or a strange, unexpected knocking coming from the attic. Something is amiss and bothering us, but we may not be sure what the cause is. If we don't listen willingly and develop the tools to pay attention, then usually pain is the initiation into the darkness of the subconscious. Just like the reflexes of the physical body, emotional and psychological pain is an alarm system forcing

TAROT THERAPY REFLECTION

Shuffle and pull three tarot cards, or journal
and discuss with a therapist or friends:
"WHAT MESSAGES IS MY SUBCONSCIOUS
COMMUNICATING AT THIS TIME?"

_____

_____

_____

_____

_____

_____

_____

_____

_____

_____

_____

us to "wake up" to ourselves. The tarot, especially in a therapeutic application, is a tool we can use to give voice and language to our subconscious, so that we don't always have to gain spiritual awareness through the difficult path of pain. Through tarot symbolism we can create a shorthand for our subconscious messages. It shows us in pictures the pieces of the puzzle we are missing.

THE SHADOW

I'm a lover of teenage occult shows. Like the majority of British-Jamaican parents, my mum was firmly against anything that made vampires and witches look appealing, and she banned me from watching *Charmed* and *Buffy the Vampire Slayer,* which she summarized as "that devil business." I sneakily watched episodes when she was out of the house and would have a decoy show ready to change the channel to if she came home unexpectedly. Now I watch them all, even though it's mostly through the gaps in my fingers as I grimace with my eyes covered!

One thing I noticed in all the occult shows I watched was that the evil twin, doppelgänger, or villain was always the better character. More compelling, more enjoyable to watch, ultimately more loved and admired (by the viewer if not by the other characters of the show). It makes me think about the subconscious self (the shadow) as not hidden and grotesque, but a possible *best self.* How can I say that, you ask? Because the shadow is true. It is the keeper of your story. Whether it pushes, rebels, and sabotages your efforts because of a conflicting deeper truth, or it reveals, teaches, and encourages you through signs and synchronicities (repeated things or events that seem to have spiritual significance), the shadow doesn't lie about who you are or what it knows. *This is why shadow work is important.* It holds the truths about us and revelations to the questions that we are seeking answers to by going on a spiritual journey.

Truth is powerful and magnetizing. It's why we love shows about sociopaths. In their refusal to tell lies that maintain social convention—which the rest of us do every day—we see a freedom we envy. It's why Joe Exotic from the documentary *Tiger King* won the empathy of many, despite being convicted of crimes of animal endangerment. In this wildly peculiar and sad story, watched by thirty-four million people, we saw something sincere in Joe. Even when horrified at his actions, as viewers, it felt like we had a very intimate view of his life. Telling the truth therefore is not just about what we say, it is about allowing ourselves to be known.

When we tell our truth we create honest bonds of connection with others. Truth, which I am distinguishing from fact (evidenced or proven), is *felt*, not known. When we hide our subconscious shadow from ourselves or others, we form connections that are only based on projections and ideas of who we are. We cheat ourselves out of true intimacy—spiritual and otherwise.

The Moon card in the tarot, then, is a depiction of the inner world. A reminder that everyone has a night, a place where the light of others cannot come. We have secret thoughts and desires, and private actions. Choosing a spiritual path is taking a journey of solitude to dive deep into ourselves to find our unique combination of desire, will, and emotion as pointing toward a truth that is uniquely ours to know.

The World

Journey, completion,
the school of life,
external influences,
lessons

The World card in the tarot represents the many different life experiences that we go through as opportunities to find the tools and lessons to put us in contact with our shadow to gain spiritual maturity. Even when we don't feel that we have good examples in our parents or communities, or we are cut off from professional help in the form of talk therapies or spiritual teachers, the world itself will always provide the conditions for growth.

The shadow pushes us toward the questions "Who are you?" and "What do you truly want?" Its intention is to bring hidden parts of you into the light for growth and development, allowing your spiritual self to be a point of connection flowing through every level of your being. In my therapeutic approach to the tarot, I interpret the four symbols of the fixed zodiac signs pictured on The World card as different cultural approaches to practicing shadow work and advancing along a spiritual journey.

These symbols are a man, a bull, a lion, and an eagle. These represent some of the ways you can personally engage in shadow work.

THE MAN

The Man is a symbol of the air element and is an expression of fixed sign Aquarius. It represents shadow work practice that specifically engages the mind for higher wisdom and understanding. This can be meditation, the study of spiritual literature, and also things like talk therapy.

Meditation prepares and creates the necessary mental quiet to "hear" the other places in our body that are speaking besides the mind. By focusing on the present, it brings us into acceptance of ourselves as we are now (essential for embracing our shadow), rather than who we were last week or might want to become tomorrow.

Through the study of religious and philosophical literature—even through the reading of this book—we can come across concepts and ideas that bring about a "light bulb moment." Something we were formerly unconscious of that suddenly connects—we see the shadow.

Talk therapies and personal storytelling assist us to sort through the habits of the mind and assess the health of our internal wiring. This is important because trauma can become a block that divides us from ourselves. The mind can compartmentalize and shut down the routes and corridors of our inner world to prioritize our immediate survival. Shadow work as an act of intentional communication helps to give us a way to "unlock" those parts of ourselves.

THE BULL

The Bull is the element of Earth and symbolizes fixed sign Taurus. This encapsulates shadow work practices that are somatic (that is, engaging the physical body and de-emphasizing the mind). This includes practices like dance and intentional movement, what we eat and drink with purpose, as well as fasting and abstinence practices.

Dance, exercise, and intentional movement (like yoga, for example) are very effective ways of transmuting energy. That means it changes the form of energy from one state to another. This is important because we know that energy cannot be destroyed. So if we are feeling an emotional state like grief, anxiety, or even love, movement gives us a way to change or express those energy states in our bodies. It can be a release through sweat or breath, for example, or an adjustment into a different feeling like calm or inspiration. Movement keeps energy flowing so that the lines of communication in the energetic body are not blocked and clogged.

We also know that what we eat and drink and the substances we come into contact with can change the body and alter our state of being. Feeling heavy, stuffed, or "grounded" after a hearty meal for example, or playful and expressive when drinking alcohol. Specific plants can have properties that alter the pathways of the mind and facilitate connection with the shadow. We can also use plant medicines to support dream states or help with pain release—physical and emotional.

Likewise, we can also abstain from particular foods or activities to induce contact with the shadow. This is one purpose of fasting, where people refrain from food and/or liquids for specific periods of time to allow the shadow to rise above the weakened appetites and urges of the physical self.

THE LION

The Lion is the element of fire and the image of fixed sign Leo. It rules the shadow work practices that have to do with challenge, confrontation, and change through direct contact or experience.

This is very much an "on the job approach" that reacts to the unexpected contact with the shadow after the fact. This is typically where the subconscious is battling or working against our conscious desires because of a conflicting inner truth. Our personal relationships are generally the terrain where this plays out. It's what is happening when we are "triggered." We may have an interaction that brings up an intense emotional or physical reaction, and it can feel compounded with other experiences from our past. Or sometimes we have no idea why we are reacting in the way we are. This is the fight club of shadow work, where we experience major challenges to our stability and power.

Usually we cope as best as we can in the moment. Afterward, in the rawness of the experience, we can come to an understanding of parts of ourselves that were not known or accessible to us before. Like when we overcome an obstacle and say, "Wow, I had no idea I could do that." Or, the discomfort of thinking, *I can't believe I said/did that*. It's the feeling that we acted "out of character" as the shadow attempts to disrupt the carefully crafted personality we show others. But this confrontation with self is just as important as the other methods of shadow work.

THE EAGLE

Finally, The Eagle is not air, as you might think, but water expressed as the fixed sign Scorpio. This is the approach to shadow work that requires the support of a guide. We can call on the wisdom and experience of elders and spiritual practitioners, or we can enlist the support of our nonphysical allies in the form of ancestors, angels, animal guides, deities, etc.

In The Eagle we are reminded to learn from the keen insights of people who have walked similar paths to us, and who demonstrate a connection with their own shadow. There is a wide range of practices that people use to develop wisdom and experience with their shadow nature and to support others in navigating their own. This includes astrology as a study of our relationship to the cosmos. Or my own favorite, the tarot, and other forms of divination practice from throwing bones and cowrie shells to reading tea leaves and palms. It refers to shamanic journeying and many other practices.

In addition to this we can work together with our spirit allies—our ancestors especially—to gain insight, revelation, and clarity. They can teach us the skills of navigating the unconscious states and use dreams, signs, and synchronicities to help us notice communications from the shadow. They help to bring balance to our physical experience so that our spiritual lives can be well placed to flourish and grow. In The World card we see that shadow work is not just one practice. It can be a combination of approaches, and what I have shared is not an exhaustive list. Though solitude is an entry point, exploration of the shadow can be a communal activity supported by connection to helpers who affirm, intervene, direct, and protect us on our spiritual journeys.

TAROT THERAPY REFLECTION

Shuffle and pull three tarot cards, or journal
and discuss with a therapist or friends:
"WHAT SHADOW WORK PRACTICES
WOULD BE BENEFICIAL TO ME?"

_____

_____

_____

_____

_____

_____

_____

_____

_____

_____

_____

_____

The Wheel of Fortune

Destiny, fate, change,
seasons, higher power,
change of luck, key, lessons

The Wheel of Fortune represents fate—the external conditions that are beyond our control and all the changes that happen in the world without our consent or active involvement. It is the promise that things will change and that life turns in cycles. If we are happy now, we will experience sadness in the future. If we are down and out now, days will come when we will feel the assistance of change lifting and supporting us. Up and down in fortune. Round and round at the promise that each of us will have moments of joy and we will all grapple with pain at times. The turning of the wheel is the cycling through the archetypal experiences that the major arcana tarot cards describe.

Along our spiritual journeys, The Wheel of Fortune teaches through repetition. It is like the saying "the more things change, the more they stay the same." In the turning of the wheel, we may encounter new experiences in life but still find ourselves in the same story. For example, realizing that you repeatedly have experiences where friends are dishonest with you. Where The Moon is about the drive toward spiritual contemplation that comes from within, The Wheel of Fortune is an external force to direct us onto a spiritual path. Illustrated with a sphinx

(Egyptian guardian of passageways) holding a sword at the top of a wheel, this card symbolizes the requirement to learn something in order to change the cycle, which will otherwise loop. Through repeating life experiences we start to question why things are happening—opening up a whole new world of spiritual exploration.

Similar to The World card, The Wheel of Fortune also has four symbols of the fixed zodiac signs and the elements: an eagle, a bull, a lion, and in this case, an angel instead of a man, representing the need to learn about our spiritual nature in order to fully realize ourselves as the developed adult pictured in The World card, the last major arcana of the tarot. Each of the beings on the card holds a book symbolizing the turning of the wheel as the school of life.

ENTRY TESTS

At the top of the card the angel and eagle represent the air (thought) and water (emotion) elements as the influence that we have to change the course of our lives. The lion and bull represent the fire (spirit) and earth (materiality) elements as things that are beyond our influence and also subject to fate. As the wheel turns it brings us to forks in the road on our spiritual journeys. As we go through our lives learning our lessons (or not) we have freedom of direction and expression about the paths we want to follow. But when the wheel turns it brings about a choice point. A moment of fate where we must prove our readiness to take the next step in our destiny (a predetermined path), or be made to repeat and contemplate other choices. This could be exemplified in the stories of people who failed at a particular talent or goal repeatedly before eventually passing. A simple personal example would be passing my driving test on the third attempt. Each time I failed, my instructor was surprised because he said I was the most capable student he had—very typical of me in my perfectionist days. I was so dismayed by failing that I wanted to give up and even sell the car I had bought prior to getting my license. The lesson I needed to break through my loop of failing my test was not technical or mechanical skill. On my third attempt, my instructor told me not to tell anyone I was taking the test and, in that secrecy, I passed. It was never a question of my ability but of freeing myself of the expectations of others. Sometimes when we feel we are not advancing in our lives it has nothing to do with our skill, worthiness, or how hard we have tried. We could be trying to be faster, smarter, or stronger when what we actually need is to let something go.

An aspect of choosing to go on a spiritual journey is learning the limitations of our free will as we realize that our lives have a scripted story. There may be lots of room for improvisation or bringing our character to life through style and aesthetic expression. As well as the joy of our costars (the people around us) and even audience engagement (messages from our spirit allies). But there are also nonnegotiable lessons and life experiences that are built into our story arc. We become stuck in loops

TAROT THERAPY REFLECTION

Shuffle and pull three tarot cards, or journal
and discuss with a therapist or friends:
"HOW CAN I BREAK FREE OF LOOPING
CYCLES ON MY JOURNEY?"

_____

_____

_____

_____

_____

_____

_____

_____

_____

_____

_____

and cycles of stagnation when we are unaware of this. It is especially the case when we try to imitate the success of others. We may see others doing really well in their respective fields and wonder why the same actions don't yield results for us. There can be structural barriers to our success, of course, but sometimes we are hitting a wall of failure that has a huge glaring U-turn sign on it. That is letting us know that there is a different story waiting for us. In spiritual communities we sometimes refer to this as "being in alignment." It is the difference between swimming upstream and being assisted by going in the with the current. Your life has a flow, a tempo, a direction. You have a destiny. When the wheel turns it helps you to feel the potential resistance of going in an counterclockwise direction.

PURPOSE

Sometimes we feel lost for a sense of purpose or personal story. This can be because we have not yet done the necessary shadow work to understand the direction of the wheel of our lives. However, sometimes it is because purpose is misrepresented by capitalism as *productivity*. When we don't know what we should be doing we sometimes mean we don't know how to be commercially successful. The success of The Wheel of Fortune is measured by our safe transition through the crossroads as significant decision-making points in our lives. Our purpose is a process of unfolding. Not only is it something we discover through the course of our lives, but we can have many life purposes. In some cases, our spiritual destiny can be entirely separate from our vocation. Where what we do for work is one of those free-will improvisations in the story of our lives—left to the discretion of our interests and pleasure.

One of the other facets of The Wheel of Fortune when it comes to purpose is its association with timing. The Moon card is about the aspect of timing that is *rhythm*. For example, the patterns of change in nature or the rhythms of change in the body (breathing in and out). However, the wheel is about the procession of time. That means there are advantageous moments to do things—*timeliness*. One of the ways we discern the creative seasons of The Wheel of Fortune (whether we are on an upward or downward swing) is through astrology. I like to think of the divine timing of The Wheel of Fortune as mirroring the astrological weather system. For example, using a Mercury retrograde as a period of time to review, edit, or change plans. Or using tarot and astrology to give particular time periods a specific purpose. For example, pulling cards for the theme of the month.

The Wheel of Fortune therefore gives us the message to trust in the promise of change and to leverage that to make a difference in the short time we have here. The things the wheel represents that are beyond our control give us focus so that we do not disperse our creative energy trying to do and be everything. By doing our shadow work and discovering the signs on our paths we are able to choose a spiritual journey that is expansive and fulfilling.

TAROT THERAPY REFLECTION

Shuffle and pull three tarot cards, or journal
and discuss with a therapist or friends:
"WHAT CAN I FIND PURPOSE IN AT THIS
STAGE OF MY LIFE?"

_____

_____

_____

_____

_____

_____

_____

_____

_____

_____

_____

_____

3

HEALING

LEARNING THE HEALING POWER OF PLEASURE AND REST

The Chariot, The Lovers, The Star

Years ago, my therapist told me to "have my cake and eat it first." Not in those exact words, but that was the sentiment. I was slumped in the chair in front of her, full of sadness. My eyes were brimming with tears as I dragged behind me the weight of all the things I felt obligated to do. She recommended that I, as an anxious insomniac overachiever, do the things I wanted to do before the things I felt I needed to do. She flipped the "work now, play later" mantra completely on its head and it led me into a practice explored by a long tradition of Black feminists from Audre Lorde to Shirley Anne Tate known as *pleasure politics*. My therapist gently nudged me to have cake for breakfast and a glass of wine with lunch if it was what I wanted, to spend hours playing computer games, and to eat Chinese food with guilt-free marathons of *Grey's Anatomy*, and this was long before a Netflix binge became a popular thing.

Having a regular nice time doesn't sound like a radical intervention. But it was less about what I was doing than what I was prioritizing: my peace. That afternoon I arrived home feeling spent from the way talk therapy requires you to pop open your mental cork and pour yourself out. So, I tried it. Instead of extending my procrastination and delaying my responsibilities indefinitely (as I feared "too much" pleasure would), allowing myself to play first made me much less resistant to facing the more difficult parts of my day.

TOO TIRED FOR JOY?

For years I had been endlessly putting off my pleasure, because I felt I had to be serious and committed. This was being driven by my perfectionist personality. Throughout my life, my self-denial masquerading as discipline was routinely rewarded as a virtue rather than a vice. I moved from one achievement to another with my anxieties only briefly satiated. That's if I was able to take pleasure in my successes at all. Most of the time I was hyper-focused on what I felt I could have done better, and so I couldn't enjoy the praise I received. Without a moment of relaxation, I was always ready to distract my inner critic with another attempt at a perfect creation. I was weary and mentally fatigued long before I had the adult responsibilities of bills and rent and bosses to contend with too.

Even as a child watching the people around me, I never

saw that hard work created lasting periods of rest or pleasure. In my working-class community, hard work was survival and everything else, especially personal relationships, had to succumb to the demands of that. "I don't have time" was the regular phrase. I don't have time to rest, or to play, or to heal; and the unspoken part: I don't have time to learn to live differently.

Following a similar path, there was a morning in my late teens when I was sitting on the bus heading to work at St. Thomas' Hospital, feeling completely stifled by my sadness. I had a data entry summer job working in patient records, and I just hated it. I knew that I was in a good position, exactly where I was supposed to be in my life by most people's estimation. It was a good and secure job that ultimately helped others, and yet I couldn't help feeling like I wanted to scream. I felt guilty, because if this was somehow not good enough for me, what did that say about the lives of others in the family? Why couldn't I accept that this was what we did to make ends meet? I told myself I was being ungrateful, and in turn that made me feel ashamed. No matter how I tried to criticize myself into submission I loathed the monotony. This is usually the part of the story with the big life-changing moment. If this were a film, then it would follow that I quit my job and by luck had the chance to get in on the ground floor of a company I always dreamed of working for. But I didn't quit. I needed the income and so I endured a miserable summer.

There was no fun purchase at the end of it. I had enough money to sustain myself and that was that. I went back to my studies plus another part-time job hoping that enduring the difficulties of hard work now would mean a pleasurable life later. I had the long-term goal of becoming an academic, teaching things I was passionate about, with a good salary and flexible hours so I could spend lots of quality time with a future partner and our babies. Spoiler alert: fast forward ten years, and while doing my PhD I found out academics were widely depressed and overworked. Constantly anxious about a schedule of writing and publishing with hardly any boundaries between work and family life, I experienced how traumatic it was to be a Black woman in higher education. Moving from a student with dreams to a staff member and researcher, the illusion dropped. I had found my passion and vocation and yet I was unwittingly still on a path taking me further and further away from rest and pleasure. Would I change direction?

The Chariot

Momentum, progress, triumph,
journey, drive, will,
desire, direction

When questioning the direction of our lives, **The Chariot card is often received as a positive sign in the tarot, indicating success on a chosen path and the likelihood of overcoming obstacles. It is a symbol of progress and momentum. But in The Chariot I also see the question: "Will we keep going until the wheels fall off?"**

Sometimes the other possible lives we could be living feel close enough that a choice or two could bridge the distance and create a much-desired change. One job application. Two good business contracts. A pregnancy, etc. But we may also find that despite our hopes, the choices we are given in life seem to only recreate the same kinds of circumstances: another overbearing manager; another relationship with fear, anger, and conflict; the same setbacks; the same hurts. In my life, I had the redirection of therapy to help break the cycle. With the additional support of tarot, I questioned what it meant to "stay on track." What would it look like to follow the path set out in front of me? Would I be happy in a life that was the fulfillment of social expectations?

My story matters because the mundane soul-crushing routines of adult life are something many of us can relate to. My weariness is definitely not the most remarkable biography you have ever heard. Lots of people have had a job they didn't love at some point. But in being quite conventional it shows the possible cost for any of us when we find ourselves stuck in our circumstances, looking out to a different, more yearned-for path. When you find yourself feeling discontented and like your life is running off track, how do you reorient it? Or do you just keep going until the "wheels fall off"? What if the wisdom of The Chariot card is having the agency to change course?

Pictured with a man forward-facing, riding high at the center of the tarot card, one of the main themes of The Chariot card is determination. It is about having a focus and strong will. To its fullest extent this can also mean a refusal to change. Riding The Chariot is about pushing forward through obstacles. But how do we reconcile this with the fact that sometimes obstacles and resistance in life are like the voice of the GPS in your car telling you to make a U-turn? It is very possible in the energy of The Chariot to go far and fast in the wrong direction. Not always because we don't know where we are headed, but because we have invested so much on this path so far, and we hope that forging ahead will mean being rewarded in the end. Sometimes changing course is a struggle with feeling like we are giving up or losing out. Or there can be serious consequences for stopping—as the speeding chariot screeches to a halt it kicks up dust and smoke, a metaphor for causing drama or making a mess with our decision. Stopping, resting, pausing, and/or turning back are actions that can be met with much resistance from ourselves and others.

CHOOSING A NEW DIRECTION

When we decide to change course in life one of the first roadblocks we encounter is a challenge to the idea that we deserve a change in the first place. We might be able to advocate to others that there are life circumstances that are making us too unwell to continue in the same direction. That we have become ill. Perhaps are struggling with depression and anxiety. Even then, in a capitalist performance-based world, what is often heard in our vulnerability is that we are *ill*-equipped. With this mindset we are en-

TAROT THERAPY REFLECTION

Shuffle and pull three tarot cards, or journal
and discuss with a therapist or friends:
"WHAT IS MY CURRENT LIFE DIRECTION,
AND WHERE AM I HEADED?"

_____

_____

_____

_____

_____

_____

_____

_____

_____

_____

_____

_____

couraged to push on with minor accommodations, like pushing through with guilt and stress to go into work when feeling sick, even though we know what we need is to be at home resting. More often than not, we give in because of responsibilities to others or the stark reality of our financial obligations.

If we can't find support to make life-changing decisions over something as critical as our mental health and well-being, it can be even harder to talk about wanting to make a life change to follow a dream or a sign of joy. At every point in my life when I have contemplated a significant change in direction, I have been met with the voices of others telling me why I can't. Or shouldn't. Or that failure is lurking down the road, waiting to embarrass me. These reservations have often been spoken with genuine concern. There are a few times I have heard the rattling of jealousy behind cautionary words. Then there were people who, though they tried, could not see the different paths I was considering, because it was just not in view from where they were standing in their lives. Over time I learned that it was not a slight to me. Especially when I watched others in my life also experience things I had not imagined could be possible when they discussed them with me. I might even have advised them against it. Sometimes we come to the crossroads alone and it doesn't matter what direction others have moved in before us. It is a unique moment to find a truth that is ours alone.

The Chariot is a card of movement. Interestingly, it

TAROT THERAPY REFLECTION

Shuffle and pull three tarot cards, or journal
and discuss with a therapist or friends:
"WHAT LIFE CHANGES COULD
I BENEFIT FROM?"

_____

_____

_____

_____

_____

_____

_____

_____

_____

_____

is uncommon to see an illustration of The Chariot that shows its momentum. It is generally a stationary image even though we understand the purpose or process of what the card does. I like to think that it is similar to the relationship between the brain and the body. Where quick signals are sent from our thoughts to create a physical action. Likewise, The Chariot is about mental clarity that makes us ready for action. This is a card about being decisive and responsive.

PLEASURE IS A GOOD REASON

In The Chariot card we are asked "What do you want?" and "Where do you want to go?" In my personal life, the more risks I took to move in the direction of the things I wanted, the more I was able to create relationships with people who shared my values. They saw my vision and validated choices that they could see would benefit me, even if they wouldn't act similarly in the same circumstances. These were family and friends who noticed what made me particularly satisfied. What I delighted in. They didn't tug me in the direction of an existing script of what a working-class Black British woman was supposed to have, or want, or be. Instead, these were people who I spent hours in deep imaginative conversations with, rerouting my life away from dead ends and exploring the possibilities of experiencing more pleasure and more peace.

Defining my life along the lines of my desires and making choices that were wholly about making myself happy was very far from the creative freedom given to previous generations. For them, the exploration of pleasure was a luxury and an infrequent indulgence otherwise reserved for luckier and wealthier people.

But pleasure is not a luxury, it is a source of power. We have talked about the charioteer, but there are always two sphinxes, horses, or other four-legged animals traditionally illustrated as pulling the chariot. Even when we have focus and conviction we also need to know what drives us. Where do we pull our power from? Shown in contrasting colors, the horses or sphinxes represent our conscious and unconscious drives. They are our impulses—like sex—and our rationale—like appreciating art and beauty. They represent the things that compel us to act. Pleasure and rest are two of our most important drives and sources of power.

When pleasure and rest are seen as superfluous in a capitalist culture of "grinding" (working hard to the exclusion of all else), it sabotages the very things we need to be creative and motivated. We don't need to earn pleasure with hard work. It is our birthright. How do we end up with the belief that our pleasure must be rationed and saved for appropriate times? That it's an indulgence that we can only have after being productive: "work now, play later"?

The Lovers

Choices, true path, destiny,
duality, love, purpose,
divine guidance

When the cultural trend is to define pleasure as a luxury (for example, expensive holidays to faraway destinations), there is one exception to this rule: that romantic relationships will satisfy the immediacy of our need for pleasure and rest. **The Lovers card in the Tarot is traditionally interpreted as a card about choices. In the popular Rider–Waite–Smith illustration there is a man and a woman, a pair of lovers, with a path laid out ahead of them and a guiding angel hovering above.** Understandably, given the imagery, many people look to this card for guidance about the experience of pleasure and romantic love in their lives. By pairing The Lovers and The Chariot cards, I am offering the reflection that our learned perceptions of love and intimacy can "lead us down a garden path" or get us off track. The promise of deep pleasure, fulfillment, and safety through romantic love is failing.

In a heteronormative society—that is, where heterosexual relationships are defined as the universal standard, with LGBTQ+ sexual orientation opposed and marginalized—women are taught from childhood to give their time, love, care, and devotion to men, in return for the promise of reciprocated feelings and protection. Men, on the other hand, are encouraged to partner for the benefits of a more productive life. With time-consuming domestic responsibility offloaded to their partners they can be freer to explore the full extent of the pleasures the world can offer them. If they are challenged or hurt on the path to getting what they want, then the relationship doubles as an emotional rehabilitation center fully stocked with enough solace to restore their pride so they can try once more.

For heterosexual women the responsibilities that come with monogamous partnering can stifle our dreams and weigh us down. Especially when there is no interrogation of the preparedness of men to meet the expectations of reciprocal love and care. Even when men are willing and desiring to, have they had life experiences up until that point that have put them in the practice of safe emotional connection and exchange, openness, and trust? Very often the answer is no because their social world is harsh, fast, pressured, and competitive. Likewise, heterosexual men are stifled in romantic partnerships by not deeply developing their relational skills through true vulnerability. It is culturally expected that the women in their lives—romantic and otherwise—who are supposedly naturally emotional, will be able to navigate the complex inner world of their emotions without men being actively engaged as a guide.

In romantic partnership especially, women will receive and hold, through sex, all the emotions that men cannot express, confront, or integrate. Women have been sold the dream of blissful and fulfilling romantic love since they were girls but, in reality, being a depository site for men's emotions is as close to affection and intimacy as many of us get.

People assume that The Lovers card is about the guided quest for true love and intimacy. It can be that. But not in the simple terms of romantic relationships between men and women. That is taken too literally. The Lovers card is about the call of the heart. It is about the choices, influences, and people on our path that help us understand not just *a truth,* but *the guiding truth of our lives.* What and who do we love, and what will we give up to commit to that path? Like the duality of the sphinxes on The Chariot, the man and woman on The Lovers also represent duality. There will always be another possible choice, another person, another direction. Love is our yes or no. It is our choice between things. The intimacy of The Lovers card is about a shared journey. The Lovers choose each other, but they can only do that when they also choose the same vision, direction, guide. This is the symbolism of the angel. The higher spiritual statute that supersedes everything. The singular choice: that the truths and decisions we live by, our personal spiritual journey, sets us on a course in life—and that road will have a set choice of lovers. People who have found their way to the same emotional, mental, or spiritual destination as you. The Lovers choose each other, but they can only do that when they also choose the same vision, direction, guide.

The idea that we will find lasting pleasure and rest through romantic love is seductive because it is so close to a spiritual truth: that is, our *need* for intimacy. But intimacy is not defined by romantic connection. In this cultural moment, many people are changing course by decentering (placing less importance on) romantic love. We are seeing that it cannot be the maximum fulfillment of pleasure in our lives—even when it is present. Having a romantic partner is not a cheat code for joy. Decentering romantic partnership is about rebalancing the overemphasis on romance as the ultimate goal and repositioning it as one of many deep intimacy needs to respond to throughout our lives.

The guidance of The Lovers card is that if we commit to ourselves, if we don't divert our lives to follow someone else, if we have the courage to choose our own direction—even when that means change—we will always move on from loneliness, dejection, and pain toward true pleasure and rest.

SHARING THE JOY

Putting off our pleasure leads to our devaluing it as something fickle. We are especially susceptible to this because we don't imagine joy, and love, and pleasure as a collective experience, but as something that is happening for someone else. Seeing the contentment of the rich and famous does not satisfy our own stomachs. Nor does watching someone else get married bring us tenderness and comfort when we are alone at night. Pleasure looks like it is a solitary benefit because of scarcity and jealousy. Because we hoard and stockpile. We curate a highlight reel online and blatantly lie or conceal the truth about unhappiness in our lives.

I realized one day that I was saving up TV shows and podcasts. Only allowing myself to listen to or watch one because I didn't want to not have something to enjoy tomorrow, or next week, or next month. Even in the smallest ways I was denying and deferring my pleasure because I did not trust that life would have more pleasure to come.

Artists are some of the sole cultural voices who remind us that there is enough pleasure for the moment we are in, and more for the next. In music we are reminded that pleasure can be a collective experience. A single expression of an artist's pleasure in a song can relay joy or resonate with hundreds of thousands of others. At its best it can be timeless, touching people in distant generations. Like hearing Roberta Flack's 1972 live performance of "The First Time I Ever Saw Your Face." Or Alice Smith's haunting and transient version of Nina Simone's song "I Put A Spell On You," originally recorded in 1964. Fifty years later, Smith took Simone's genius and imbued it with such presence that it is like a beautiful trance every time I hear it. Through the artists of each era, we join in the pleasure of finding ourselves held and understood. This is the intimacy of The Lovers card. In the artists we love, we meet on a path connecting through their art. In the company of their work, it is like we are hitchhiking partway along our journey, sharing someone else's vision and seeing something beautiful.

Even if it is not the example of the unique euphoria of a virtuoso's song, how many times have we watched the best show or film we have ever seen, only to find more and more delight in something that comes next? *Interstellar*, *True Grit*, *Lovecraft Country*, *Get Out*, *Moonlight*, *Schitt's Creek*, *The Office (US)*, *The Good Wife*, *Queen Sugar*, *Snowfall*, *The Expanse*, *Battlestar Galactica*, *Wanda-Vision*, *Watchmen*, *City of God*, *Hunter x Hunter*, *Train to Busan*, *Parasite*, *Squid Game*. I could go on and on in my list of amazing TV shows and films that I thought to myself while watching, *I love this so much, I'm so happy.* That's not counting the good, and the so-bad-it's-almost-good, things I have seen.

Perhaps this is why the cinema became my favorite place to retreat to. I would take entire meals in with me: Nando's chicken in pitta, PERi-PERi chips, and a bottle of cider to accompany two hours of blissful fantasy. Again and again. Similar to the pleasure I have derived from the creativity of others in film, TV, and music, the things we do that light us up are like a personal sun that makes a summer for ourselves and the people around us. Pleasure is a source of life.

TAROT THERAPY REFLECTION

Shuffle and pull three tarot cards, or journal
and discuss with a therapist or friends:
"WHAT WAYS AM I A PLEASURE TO BE
AROUND IN THE EYES OF OTHERS?"

_____

_____

_____

_____

_____

_____

_____

_____

_____

_____

_____

The Star

Vision, renewal, rest,
hope, health, inspiration,
creativity, divine connection

In The Star card we pause, we stop, we rest. This is a sacred pleasure that is the nature of the journey itself. Rest is not a reward. It does not come after hard work or any other means of earning it. We rest because every other important thing in our lives is dependent on it. Pictured as a woman—the water bearer as symbol of Aquarius—bathed in starlight and connected to the sea and the land. A reminder of the balance that the night, sleep, and dreams bring. During this time, the physical self surrenders to the subconscious, and the world of the spirit, as it balances and restores us. In turn, on waking, the spirit surrenders to the conscious rational self to animate and perform the dreams and deep desires conveyed while asleep. Round and round in a reciprocal partnership of self-care and creativity.

Just as we look to our spiritual path to provide us with new creative possibilities, so the duality of The Star offers us practices as a response to the questions posed by The Chariot and The Lovers. The Star as card seventeen is literally and figuratively ten steps ahead in its message.

What The Star primarily teaches us is that rest is not optional. It is the only way to be attuned to life. It is also not just limited to time spent sleeping; rest isn't just a

TAROT THERAPY REFLECTION

Shuffle and pull three tarot cards, or journal
and discuss with a therapist or friends:
"WHAT IS A SIGN FOR ME TO NOTICE
WHEN IT IS TIME FOR ME TO REST?"

_____

_____

_____

_____

_____

_____

_____

_____

_____

_____

_____

_____

practice of non-movement—it implies a temporary pause before returning to something. Therefore, rest is a practice of recalibration—resetting the levels. Sometimes it is a cultural reset at the level of our belief systems. At other times it can be a pause from questioning and seeking to allow what has been present up to this point to settle.

There are ways of resting that are active. For me, that is how I experience my computer games. I can spend ten hours on *Tropico* or *Cities: Skylines* designing a city right down to the most minor detail. Even though I am mentally focused and engaged when I'm playing, it gives me space for creative expression and relaxed problem-solving. It's a break from mental pressures that have serious real-world consequences. Rest can mean to refrain from something—like social media or a busy city environment—but rest can also be the addition of something nourishing, like a physical movement practice, or for me: gaming.

YOU HAVE ENOUGH TIME

Many spiritual traditions across the world encourage the merits of slowing down and "being present" as a form of focused awareness often referred to as "mindfulness." But can we rest or be mindful when we are trying to keep up with the pressures of life? When perhaps some of us are anxiously focused on the basics of survival, like covering the rent?

The figure in the The Star card is alone, her nakedness

suggests safety and vulnerability. If we're not in places of physical or emotional safety, then rest is not only difficult, letting our guard down could also be dangerous. Only from a place of safety can rest transform into pleasure. If we are not actually physically or emotionally safe, then in this context rest must be thought of as the freedom from the fear of disaster. Rest in this instance is to create or find temporary space, support, and respite until we are able to make it to safety.

Our body is a primary place where we need to experience safety. But we cannot assume that all people are able to "come back to the body" (as many emotional-wellness-centered movement practices encourage) to rest and feel pleasure; this can be disrupted by shame, physical trauma, chronic pain, etc. Rest is about the transformation of environments—bodies and societies—to become hospitable to our primary need to stop.

In The Star card, having to pause things is a gift rather than a disappointment. It is a reprieve, with the knowledge that we can and will continue. It allows us to check our direction, to look at the stars in relation to our inner compass. We can take stock of our resources and our wellness. *Will we keep our chariot going until the wheels fall off?*

In the focus of the night we can find clarity about the things that are important to us for the long-term. The things that will matter today and tomorrow and next year and beyond. In the two cups of The Star card we can learn the reciprocity of pouring lovingly into ourselves (sea), and into communities that bloom like gardens (land) that many will take shelter in and be nourished by for years to come; healing and pleasure-filled legacies that will outlive us.

4

CHANGE

Living with Change and
Losing Control

Death, The Tower, The Hanged Man

I am someone who loathes routine. It's why self-employment has brought me so much pleasure and fulfillment, because I can vary my days and hours. Though it's also why I kept becoming exhausted! With all that freedom I was constantly picking up new projects of interest and then finding myself overwhelmed. I love small-scale change, like the opening of a new restaurant or discovering previously unknown routes of exploration in my local area. But when it comes to bigger life changes, I have probably been more resistant and fearful than the average person—or perhaps I'm just being hard on myself! Still, there are two instances in my life where I struggled to cope with major change and delayed the blessings and freedoms that eventually came.

I have shared parts of these personal stories throughout this book. The first was having the courage to leave the church I had gone to for twelve years from the age of seven—the formative years in my life. I was miserable, hurt, and having recurring nightmares about being there for two years before I faced the conflict of saying I wanted to explore my faith in other places. The second experience was painfully wrestling with myself over quitting my PhD. This is one of the hardest choices I have ever made because it was the path I had strived for, for more than a decade. Was I just going to give up with no final accolade or qualification to show for that time? I still remember a meeting I had with a trusted professor who, seeing me torn, asked me what my reason for doing the PhD was. I told him I had always wanted to write a book and that my thesis was the message I wanted to share with my community. He told me I didn't need a PhD to be an author. At that time, it was the only clear path available to me, but when I eventually decided to stop my research, I grieved the dream of being an author as something that would not happen for me. Yet here I am telling you this story in my first book. This is the beauty of change even when we feel like we are losing control of our dreams or our path.

In the past couple of years, living abroad has challenged my sense of control and the idea that I know what will happen and am sure of the experiences that are best for me. I often didn't know what country I would be in or for how long. While elements of living abroad have been stressful, I have now started to see without having my 100-step plan detailing half the coming year by January 1. I can see life turning out in ways that are better than I imagined. Powerful and productive change is not just in the big moments. It's also the gradual shifts we make as we embrace life lessons. For me, this was becoming the happiest and safest I had ever felt. Without actually knowing in advance *how* those positive changes would come about for me. Embracing change with more ease is an act of having faith.

THE THREE FACES OF CHANGE

When we become spiritually mature enough to observe the story of our life unfolding and the repeated patterns, lessons, and mistakes that emerge, it is a common response to want to take control. This is what we call coming into conscious awareness, where we move away from the feeling that things happen *to us*, toward a sense of *agency* by defining who we want to be and making changes to steer our lives in the direction of our vision and desires. This is usually the point when people consider the question of free will versus fate. How much of our lives can we truly have power over, and what is beyond the limits of our influence? Either in the form of other powerful agents (governments and authority figures, for example), or in the form of a higher power that sets the obstacle course of our life path. Do the choices we make really bring change, or are we destined to follow a certain life trajectory no matter what we do, like actors playing out a predetermined script? The answer to that question is different for everyone. The question posed is: what can I truly change?

The major arcana cards Death, The Tower, and The Hanged Man are three faces of change that we encounter throughout our lives. Each of them teaches us to relate to the power of change differently. Death ushers us into new phases of life, and though this can happen with pain and loss, it can include things that are joyful, such as birth or marriage. The Tower represents change that comes through shock or psychological breakthrough. It is about crisis and struggle. This archetype represents being startled into adaptability and creative problem-solving through moments of intensity. By contrast, The Hanged Man is about being subjected to conditions we *cannot change*. This position drives an internal rather than external transformation. By using the tarot we can recognize these stages of transition and support ourselves in navigating these different turning points in our lives. Even when we most want things to remain the same, change is essential to our capacity to heal, grow, and stay connected in relationships with others. We must learn to discern between boundaries of our influence and control and find acceptance within the larger cycles of change in our lives.

TAROT THERAPY REFLECTION

Shuffle and pull three tarot cards, or journal
and discuss with a therapist or friends:
"WHAT LIFE CHANGES AM I STRUGGLING
TO ACCEPT?"

_____

_____

_____

_____

_____

_____

_____

_____

_____

_____

_____

_____

Death

Endings, change, departure,
release, rebirth, cycle,
ancestors, ghosts, grim reaper

Alongside The Devil, the Death card in the tarot creates the most unease for novices during a tarot reading. Even for the more experienced, its presence often indicates an unwanted conclusion. **We know that something is or will be over and there will be no choice but to let go. Death brings harsh and uncompromising truths.** Typically pictured as a grim reaper figure riding through a scene of destruction, the Death card is not a happy scene. Even when representing something we want to end—like the conclusion of a difficult legal battle—death is costly. We are losing something. It could be money or a relationship or even an old version of ourselves; finding that we are decidedly different having gone through this change. As a tarot archetype Death symbolizes the events and actions that interrupt our expectations of life. As a metaphor it represents completions and final endings that mean something ceases to be, and something else comes into existence in its place.

Though Death rarely means a fatality in the context of a tarot reading, it is associated with mortality. As the idiom goes, "the only constant thing in life is change" and death is the ultimate fulfillment of this. All of us know that we will die and that is the inevitable conclusion to life. Some people suggest living as though each day were our last, but if we really lived staring into the gaping abyss of the unknown, imagining ourselves being swallowed up by death, we would never do anything.

Being alive requires us to forget. To take our end for granted and imagine a thousand more tomorrows as we sign work contracts, book holidays, and have children. Our willful ignorance of the clock that ticks away our unknown allotted time is how we become engrossed in our terrestrial nature—earth is what we know and this is where we live. So, when someone dies or when something comes to an end, it disrupts the normality of life and pushes back into view the bigger picture that this planet and this life are a very small part of a vast expanse. We suddenly have to consider ourselves within the scale of it all, what our lives might mean as we make an approach toward our own promised end.

ENDINGS AND NEW BEGINNINGS

From a spiritual perspective, the change that Death brings is a process of *initiation*. It has the power to awaken us, similar to the way pain sharpens the senses and gives a sudden increase in awareness. Take, for example, burning yourself while cooking (as I do often) and your sudden reflex to move away from the source of the heat. That pain makes you aware of your body and your surroundings. In the same way, the pain that we experience when we are confronted with a death stage in our lives (a sense of emptiness, loss, something we're attached to being taken away, the end of pleasure) brings us back into awareness about where we are and where we want to go.

Death is a fork in the road for the living. It can be the reason someone takes a risk to go after a long-held dream. Or even to give up the pursuit of a dream denied to focus on the values that have suddenly come into sharp focus. This could be leaving a job, moving back to a hometown, or spending more time with friends. Death is one of the critical moments where we consider our overall direction as explored through The Chariot card in chapter 3.

Another key aspect of the Death tarot card is separation: the purpose of the grim reaper is to sever. The endings entailed by the Death card are often about spanning an unbridgeable distance. When someone dies, we know our physical contact with them ceases. But there are other kinds of endings that keep us apart from people, places, and things. This is about an experience you can never make tangible again. Take, for example, a married couple who are estranged, get divorced, reunite, and remarry. Even though they come back together, they can never again have the version of their marriage that existed before the divorce. They are at a permanent separation from those versions of themselves and the life they created. They can have something new, but they are forever altered. Even if they play out a similar drama and repeat their mistakes. Each cycle through an experience is different. In the example of the reconciled couple, a repeated pattern may hurt more deeply, or escalate more

TAROT THERAPY REFLECTION

Shuffle and pull three tarot cards, or journal
and discuss with a therapist or friends:
"HOW CAN I FIND INSPIRATION IN THE
THINGS THAT ARE ENDING?"

_____

_____

_____

_____

_____

_____

_____

_____

_____

_____

quickly, etc. Even if in this new cycle they love each other well, they will do so having to tend to the pains of the past. They can never be brand-new lovers again.

In a different example, we can consider the end of our primary school years. I often hear people remark on how much they cried on that last day. I have memories of crying through my school assembly, clutching my friends in hugs, and having everyone write parting messages in permanent marker on my white school shirt. I have no idea where that shirt is now, but it was a beautiful rite of passage nonetheless. The severance of death here is the end of childhood. There is no going back. I can never again be ten years old with a crush on the most popular boy in class. Or make up dances to pop songs in the playground. Those days are gone forever.

When something ends, we often have to cope with the discomfort of unfamiliarity and feelings of aloneness. But in the process of separation and loss we also come up with a new vision because we have no other choice. This is the gift of the Death card, it brings the kind of change that moves us forward.

TAROT THERAPY REFLECTION

Shuffle and pull three tarot cards, or journal
and discuss with a therapist or friends:
"WHAT IS NOW POSSIBLE FOLLOWING
THE LOSSES I HAVE ENCOUNTERED?"

_____

_____

_____

_____

_____

_____

_____

_____

_____

_____

_____

_____

The Tower

Shock, power struggle,
crisis, breakthrough,
destruction, chaos, news

We don't always make radical changes after something difficult. Sometimes we make ourselves promises (to take our health more seriously, for example) but ultimately get seduced back into the comfortable routines of life and the status quo. **The Tower card in the tarot is one of the cards I like to call *The Hand of God*. It is one of the few instances where the meaning has nothing to do with executing our power or agency at all. The Tower comes when we are stuck, often unknowingly. It is the destruction of our comfort zones and tendency to coast.**

Illustrated as a shocking scene of a bolt of lightning hitting a tower and causing it to crumble, people flying through the windows and downward toward their presumed death (change), The Tower is a force of destruction. But the lightning as the alarming instrument of the divine does not directly hit the people—it could, but it decisively hits the building instead, showing that The Tower is a force of liberation. The collapse of the tower is the act of freeing us from the beliefs and life situations that are causing us to be trapped or stuck.

The liberatory power of The Tower is not just moving us from one place to another though. Its collapse can

TAROT THERAPY REFLECTION

Shuffle and pull three tarot cards, or journal
and discuss with a therapist or friends:
"WHAT SHOCKING OR NEW
INFORMATION IS BRINGING
CHANGE INTO MY LIFE?"

_____

_____

_____

_____

_____

_____

_____

_____

_____

_____

_____

_____

_____

represent a mental and emotional crisis or breakdown. It is to lose our sense of order or security. To be plunged into chaos, fear, and confusion. Lightning as a symbol of sudden illumination gives The Tower card a connotation of shocking news or information. When this card appears in a reading it is because we have recently had, or are about to have, our worlds rocked.

A shock can be finding out you are being evicted and only have three days to move and find somewhere else to live. Or being told the company you work for is relocating and you have to move cities and drastically uproot your life or lose your job. The Tower brings unexpected change. I have given extreme and dramatic examples here, but the things that shake your world will be different for each person. The tower is about psychological response to external change. It tends to refer to bigger moments in life, but it can just as easily be news that makes us *fearful* of what *could* happen next. Each of our stress thresholds are different. Being told I missed my flight home, for example, definitely felt like a Tower moment for me. In other circumstances, The Tower can be realizing we are not over something we thought we had already emotionally processed. Like another wave of hurt or loss as a psychological flood of emotions.

TAROT THERAPY REFLECTION

Shuffle and pull three tarot cards, or journal
and discuss with a therapist or friends:
"WHAT CAN I SEE NOW THAT I
COULDN'T SEE BEFORE?"

_____

_____

_____

_____

_____

_____

_____

_____

_____

_____

_____

_____

WHAT NEXT?

The Tower brings mental stress for the purpose of break-through. It requires us to problem-solve on a very tight deadline. It is a situation of extremes where we are challenged to adapt fast. The Tower often appears when we cannot be reasoned with. When we've missed more subtle signs and red flags. It's like a messenger who isn't going to make it to you in time, so they throw a grenade nearby instead and that gets your attention. The Tower is not an eloquent teacher—it is a lesson of immediacy. You have to think fast to understand: What in your life is on fire now? What do you need to cut out or get away from? Who or what do you have toxic bonds to?

I am very familiar with the power of the Tower card. It is a force that moves us along even if we have not rested or recovered enough to do so. We are forced to make it through the next part of our lives with injuries. We must metaphorically run with a broken leg. Or, in my case, complete important creative projects while utterly heart-broken and dejected.

The Tower is an act of divine intervention. Some might see it as dramatic interference! More than any other card, I find The Tower follows a cosmic pattern. It is common to feel the power and energy of The Tower around eclipses, for example. There was a popular TV show on the SYFY channel called *The Magicians* that was a very enjoyable binge watch for me. There was one idea from that show that I have held on to as an important life lesson: knowing the internal and external conditions for performing a magic trick. That is, there are things that you can control and set up (internal conditions), and then there are environmental factors like the time of day or the weather, etc. (external conditions). The Tower to me is one of those external conditions. It's like a build-up of tension until a critical point is reached and then suddenly a lightning bolt of revelation strikes. During this time our internal conditions have also been aligning (mind, body, emotions), gradually making us ready to broaden our perspective. That is, we get the lesson of The Tower because we are finally ready to understand it.

There is some comfort in this; that realizations will always be forthcoming. That even when we are at our most stuck, or obstinate or clueless, life itself will conspire to show us what we need to see. Of course, we don't always want to learn through shock and horror; that can be traumatic. But even if we have to learn the extremely hard way, there is a peace in knowing that we are never lost causes. That life as a divine instructor never stops teaching.

Life changes that happen through the energy of The Tower typically stretch us. We look back on those times as moments of great pressure where we rose to the challenge and showed greater strength than we knew we had. The Tower as an agent of change brings us rapid personal growth.

TAROT THERAPY REFLECTION

Shuffle and pull three tarot cards, or journal
and discuss with a therapist or friends:
"WHAT AM I CURRENTLY FINDING
TEDIOUS? WHAT DO I WANT TO
CHANGE?"

_____

_____

_____

_____

_____

_____

_____

_____

_____

_____

The Hanged Man

*Pause, reflection, sacrifice,
change in perspective,
surrender, release*

In the Hanged Man card we are confronted with things in our lives that are very slow to change. This major arcana card is one of the most important symbols of patience. It shows a person hanging upside down from a tree with a halo of light surrounding their head. In this card we pause for reflection. But introspection is a common theme throughout the tarot as it is a journey we take within, or through the mind, so to speak. What distinguishes the contemplation of The Hanged Man from other tarot cards is the upside-down suspension: to look at something from a completely different angle. There is an inherent stillness in this card. It does not have the movement of The Hermit or the preaching words of The Hierophant, both of which we'll be introduced to in the next chapter. The act of suspension is surrender. It is to accept circumstances as they are without forcing an external change. In The Hanged Man, we attempt to change ourselves by seeing things differently.

Out of all three faces of change, The Hanged Man can be uniquely challenging because it isn't energizing in the same way as Death or The Tower. Those experiences are kinetic. They involve movement and action and catalyzing moments. By contrast, The Hanged Man is about

TAROT THERAPY REFLECTION

Shuffle and pull three tarot cards, or journal
and discuss with a therapist or friends:
"WHAT SIGNS AND SYMBOLS ARE
ASSISTING ME WITH THE THINGS I FEEL I
CANNOT CHANGE?"

_____

_____

_____

_____

_____

_____

_____

_____

_____

_____

circumstances that endure. Things that are literally held in place. It can be the excruciating passage of time. Dealing with the *unchanging* nature of something when we would rather have things be otherwise. These are the occasions where we rush to move on from difficult emotions because we want that stage of our lives to be over, but we find ourselves having to endure the different stages of experiencing and expressing our feelings.

CHANGED BY RESPONSIBILITY

An example that affects many families is co-parenting with someone you have a great deal of conflict with. Their biological connection to your child as a parent will not change, no matter how much you might have regrets and wish otherwise. It is a fixed reality. The dynamic of the co-parenting relationship is an aspect that could change, however. But being dependent on the character, wisdom, and will of multiple parties, it is likely to be the very slow unfolding of change over time that The Hanged Man characterizes. You have absolutely no control over the actions of the other parent (except where legal limitations have been placed). Therefore, you have to surrender to the reality of your co-parenting situation. The same applies if you are dealing with an absentee parent. In both instances, you become The Hanged Man. Tied to the circumstances, your only choice is to struggle against the facts or turn yourself upside down, see the situation from a new angle, and find new approaches to parenting that benefit the overall well-being of your family. The influence of The Hanged Man is to slowly develop you through the pressure of fixed circumstances. In this example, perhaps you become better at communicating with the other parent. Or you find new strategies for giving your child a sense of comfort and connection when they express sadness and longing for their other parent. Maybe the parenting journey exposes your wounds and insecurities and gives you room to heal and to also parent yourself in the areas you felt that care was missing. All of this is part of the purview of The Hanged Man.

The Hanged Man invites us into a low-pressure process of confrontation by keeping us tied to things we would rather walk away from. If we ran away from every uncomfortable situation and avoided all our responsibilities, we would never grow. Think of it in exercise terms as the strength gained from holding a pose. The Hanged Man can be slow and unyielding, but it is beneficial.

YOUR CHOICE

Unlike the other types of change, The Hanged Man experience is often a choice or something we understand our role and participation in. The seclusion of the Hanged Man card is voluntary. The person pictured in the card has climbed the tree themselves and they are free to come down whenever they choose to. The solitary nature of this card can therefore be a space to receive dreams and visions that support The Hanged Man in gaining under-standing. Spiritual insight and inspiration is signified by an illustration of the halo of enlightenment.

The Hanged Man can be very empowering in the clar-ity and perspective it brings. This is also because it in-volves a willing sacrifice. We may give up our comfort to engage in this process. We may also surrender our sense of power by not exerting control or seeking to push for a change. But, in return, we experience a different kind of power: peace and self-discipline.

The Hanged Man is one of the most powerful influ-ences of change because what changes internally has the potential to reflect a radically new world of possibilities for us. The experiences we have are not solely dependent on us. It isn't all manifestation and law of attraction. The societies we live in are cocreated and involve the actions and thoughts and intentions of many different beings—and not just human beings; we can include the plant world and animal kingdom in this. However, the parts of our lives that are the result of our thoughts and actions can be radically transformed by the inner transformations of the Hanged Man. We can experience the reconciliation of inner conflicts through shifts in perspective.

When my parental relationships broke down, I spent a long time feeling abandoned and rejected by them. My struggle with these emotions was definitely the main subject of my years in talk therapy. But in a moment of introspec-tion when I was living in a very uncomfortable situation that I could not change, I had a sudden and profound realization: I was not abandoned. I walked away. I could have relationships with my parents if I wanted to. Yes, they would be wounding and disempowering for me. But the choice was there. I had chosen differently. I had made a powerful decision of self-love and preservation. That adjustment of events in my mind meant that at the next birthday of a parent—a time that is usually full of sadness for me—I was peaceful for the first time. I was free. That internal change also affected all my other relationships, allowing me to show up more open and less burdened by feelings of fear and unworthiness.

GRACEFUL CHANGES

Whatever direction the influence of change is taking you in—the completion of things, the push into a new direction, or a restriction on your freedom—the main thing I want you to consider is how to go through these changes with the least amount of suffering. Change is often painful. This is true. But suffering comes from being torn and twisted, from resistance and confusion and struggle. At any given time, consider these three forces of change as a guide and aid to you. Trust yourself to come through your changes whole. The transitional corridors of change can be difficult, and this is when we most need to be gentle and compassionate with ourselves. This is when we need a deep practice of kindness to draw from and nourish and strengthen ourselves. No matter what comes or goes in the revolving door of change, it is most important that we stay. That we do not abandon ourselves by giving up or refusing to give ourselves care or seek out support. You are the true constant. Regardless of the changing faces in your life, don't forget to truly see the beauty of your own journey.

5

TRUTH

Claiming Your Wisdom in
a World of Strong Opinions

The Hermit, The Hierophant, The Fool

As a child I was always told I talked too much. I was blogging at the height of Myspace and writing short stories, poetry, and songs before I was even a teen. Now I am a "spend hours on the phone talking to a friend" and "write paragraphs to the man I love about the way I feel" kind of woman. I have always had something to say. Always cared deeply. Always advocated and debated. Until recently.

I lost my voice. I can't write about truth, wisdom, and strong opinions without also being honest about that. In the last few years, I lost my passion for life and fell into a silence, feeling disappointed and uninspired. I want to say I don't know how it happened, how I became so quiet, insular, and sullen, but I do: I found myself on a love journey that would turn my life upside down, and in that process lead me to my wisdom. The challenge I faced was to vanquish the hovering judgments and opinions of others. There were many times I failed at that, echoing their fear or muting myself entirely. *I was ashamed of my truth because I was different.*

I write these words for the parts of you that you have felt you have had to hide from the world. For the days and months that are full of doubt and confusion. This is my way of signposting the road of wisdom and steering you clear of the ditches and dangers that wounded me. This is a story about me having had my heart broken; telling it is like excavating my voice from the debris.

A JOURNEY INTO SILENCE

After many painful failures in love I had taken a long break from dating to heal and focus on myself. For an entire year I went to bed at night repeating a simple prayer: that I was lonely, but so grateful that nobody's son was breaking my heart. It was a prayer of genuine gratitude and relief. An affirmation to myself that celibacy was the right choice for me. When I was feeling confident enough again and ready to date, I decided to focus on having fun and being lighthearted. *I didn't expect to meet a soulmate.*

I had always believed *true love* would be easy, that it would feel like a synchronous dance. I hadn't the slightest clue that spiritual love could feel much more like a brutal fight to the death. That rather than being a source of ease and comfort, some spiritual relationships had the purpose of bringing uncomfortable realizations. Truths about ourselves we would otherwise not face up to. That the vulnerability and exposure of a spiritual love could turn intimacy into an open field of landmines for our emotional triggers. A dramatic form of spiritual awakening that dredges up your repressed memories and feelings, and sends them rippling toward you across the murky lake of a love so special you had been eager to dive into it. When love unexpectedly connects you to your subconscious depths, it can feel like you are drowning.

In the beginning, with this soulmate, there was no hint that feeling drawn to each other would be a painful catalyst of life changes. The first time we met we were seated in a cozy pub restaurant and talked for hours about everything and anything. We stayed until closing and I feared perhaps he wasn't really into me; it had all been so friendly with minimal flirting from him. But right before we parted ways, he kissed me. I smile whenever I think of it. I remember thinking, *This is my person.* Months later it was the Easter holidays (a festive period I much preferred to Christmas) and I was completely in love. I asked him to make time for me, and later that evening I was next to him, tracing his fading tattoos with my fingertips. As night approached he clambered over to turn off the bedroom light and came back folding me deep into a hug. "Why do you like to be in my arms so much?" he asked. The answer then, though I didn't say it to him, has been the truth every day since: love to me is *home,* and to be without it is to be in exile.

AN UNWANTED ENDING

I had been in love three times before him. For real. I mean the kind of love still validated by the benefit of hindsight and retrospect. On my worst days, those men still appear in my dreams like a placebo for my heart. Reminding me of times of trust, care, and comfort. I consider them soulmates too; the agreeable kind sent to be sweet and safe temporary companions for parts of your life. This love was different. It was intoxicating and addictive. A pull like nothing I had felt before.

It was the winter in the year after we had met when he said our love was so much bigger and deeper, much more than he expected or even wanted at that point in his life. When he ended things, it fractured me. My mind was splitting at the seams. I was confused that the forever of this love, a miracle of the heart, was contradicted by an ending. I stayed in bed, drank Prosecco, and binge-watched all four epic seasons of *Battlestar Galactica*. After weeks, I was not even marginally soothed. I ached and reached out to him over and over again; a repeated three-month cycle of forcing myself to move on, feeling stuck, and running back, until eventually he ghosted me completely. The heartache I felt would go on to isolate me for years. I had to survive it somehow, and I found strength in the consuming focus of my PhD work. I split my heart and my mind to survive. I focused on mentally taxing tasks that didn't require me to feel anything, passing the time with productive distractions. That is until, still stuck in my grief and searching for answers, I got interested in the tarot.

I was struggling with feeling ashamed of the fact that distance and time had not loosened his hold on my heart. Through the tarot I began to ask questions and explore the inextricable connection I felt to him. But no matter how many times tarot readings echoed back the power and purpose of my love, I still hid and silenced myself. Who would understand? Trying to talk to friends and loved ones about it left me feeling disoriented and dejected as they overruled what I was feeling to give me "tough love." Or they showed compassion but were just as lost as me about what I needed to do to *move on*. I became a half self. This time, I split up my life into things I could and could not talk about, parts of me I would and wouldn't show.

Even in my closest familial relationships I omitted parts of me, and not being fully seen for who I was, I was waning. My relationships were imbalanced. I listened, loved, and supported, and that's how I felt valid and connected to others. But I could not risk the intimacy and honesty needed to receive the same in return. This meant disappearances and "I just need some time to myself" messages from myself to others when I was struggling the most. I was sinking deeper and deeper into my self-imposed prison. I felt so locked in until that part of me just gave up on trying to speak.

TAROT THERAPY REFLECTION

Shuffle and pull three tarot cards, or journal
and discuss with a therapist or friends:
"IN WHAT WAYS DO I SILENCE MYSELF?"

_____

_____

_____

_____

_____

_____

_____

_____

_____

_____

_____

THE BODY KEEPS SECRETS

For two years I had extreme pain that would fill the right side of my chest as a physical expression of profound grief. At the very worst of it, I called a friend in floods of tears after fearing I was having a heart attack when a sharp pain ricocheted through my chest while I was lifting groceries. The pain in my body was real and dangerous; but the cause of the concrete wall forming around my heart was not physical. This is referred to as *psychosomatic*: I was sick in my body because of the struggle in my thoughts. I booked a body massage to help manage the pain and my feelings of abandonment and neglect.

I traveled to Lisbon, Portugal, to get away from London in search of my peace. I discovered there was an energy healer working from a massage shop that was next door to the apartment I was staying in. It was fortuitous because, for me, the same person who had traveled across countries, getting out of bed was still too hard on some days. At my saddest, going next door felt just about doable so I booked it. The masseur asked to speak to me after our very first session and said, "The right side of your chest, so much pain, so blocked." In a mix of Portuguese and English he told me that the energy center in my stomach was overloaded because my heart was broken. He knew nothing about me, but the truth was in my body. The chest pain that had affected me for years never fully left until the day he—this great love of mine—and I spoke again. In that conversation he gave me a truth; something

I had been deeply convinced of and yet too afraid to fully trust without proof. He told me he had also been hurt and miserable during those years apart. That during that time he had never stopped feeling connected to me or noticing the spiritual signs that pointed him back in my direction. We talked for hours about how we had changed and what we had both learned on our separate paths, and what we would mean to each other going forward.

There are consequences for silencing ourselves. I reflect back on those years and see that I did not know how to give myself grace. I did everything the hard way. I took our divergent paths to mean I was wrong; that we could not have been soulmates. All I could see was that I was stuck in a ghost story feeling and seeing him everywhere. The more my intuition grew, the more impossible it became to ignore. I would know things about his life without him telling me, sense his emotional state whenever there was an extreme. The gift I was using to intuitively guide and support others with tarot was also the very thing keeping me connected to him. I even tried at times to give that up. Shut down all my spiritual gifts. I questioned if I was going crazy. Why was my intuition constantly directing me back to a path I thought was a dead end?

I was exhausted to the bone and dejected by my feelings of being exiled from love. The sorrow almost ended me for one reason: *I could not accept or tell my truth.* It didn't actually matter whether others believed or understood my connection to him. Not at that point. Those deep and sacred spiritual friendships would come later. The thing that was stifling the life out of me was that

I refused to believe myself. It is one thing to trust your gut or intuition over something you want; something you believe you can have. But to listen to your inner wisdom when logic and cold hard facts say nothing could come of it? That kind of faith is rare.

I had tried everything to evict him from my heart. Until my radical act of self-preservation was to put all my belongings in storage and get on a plane to start over, hoping to finally leave behind the ghosts of our love and the life I had wanted with him. The world was beautiful: Brazil, Mexico, South Africa. I was happier than I had been in years . . . *and I missed him.* This love was relentless and unending and only inflamed by my continuous struggle to deny it. A trusted peer gave me a tarot reading and cautioned me that my emotional habit was to allow waves of feeling to break me against rocks. The struggle was too much. She was right. For three years I was at war with myself over love. I was stuck because I wasn't fully heeding my inner wisdom in the midst of other strong opinions. Even when those critical and unforgiving opinions were my own.

The Hermit

Contemplation, solitude, withdrawal,
exploring the unknown, discovery,
faith in the journey, wisdom

There are many ways we silence ourselves, negate, deny, and hide. Reasons we make ourselves small. Or play into what is expected of us; exaggerate or flat-out lie. We all conform at times as the cost of belonging, but living in our truth requires "main character" thinking. It is recognizing that the incomplete script of our life stories is being written daily through our thoughts, emotions, and actions. If we can't express our truths with our lives then we censor ourselves into a vanilla and respectable performance for the satisfaction of others. **The Hermit in the tarot is the complete rejection of this audience. I like to think of the aged depiction of The Hermit as having grown tired of the spectacle of having to prove the merit of our lives to others.**

The Hermit is illustrated as an old and solitary figure in simple clothing, carrying a staff and lantern through a bleak landscape. The intention of The Hermit is to minimize external influences. To enter a period of contemplation for the pursuit of wisdom. Reading tarot for ourselves, for example, is a way of experiencing (if only for short periods of time) the contemplative seclusion of The Hermit in our modern lives. One of the sacred gifts of the tarot is its ability to put us back in touch with our own voice and intuition when we are lost in the influence of the opinions and perceptions of others. Especially when our internal mental voice becomes indistinguishable from the voices of our parents, advisers, or friends. Like hearing their words at each turn as a running commentary on our choices.

Having trouble communicating a personal truth, or even acknowledging it inwardly, is one of the most common spiritual blocks I find when reading tarot for clients. Despite the many sources of knowledge available to us through the expansion of the internet, I regularly support people who are completely overwhelmed without a sense of life direction or of what choices could be right for them. Having more information does not automatically result in making us wiser. One of the core aspects of The Hermit archetype is to use what is already known to cast light on the paths through life presently available to us. To The Hermit, wisdom is not just what we are taught but how we develop our own ways of gaining knowledge of the world. Right or wrong, The Hermit commits to choosing a direction, seeing what experience comes out of the journey into the unknown.

Often, we are too afraid of being wrong or too afraid of facing failure to take action in our lives without having a (false) sense of control, or a promise of certainty and security. We want to deal in absolutes and we often derive this through the agreement and affirmation of others: from our romantic partners, peer groups, employers, etc. Sometimes we draw confidence indirectly by following the example of people around us and seeking to replicate the blueprint of

TAROT THERAPY REFLECTION

Shuffle and pull three tarot cards, or journal
and discuss with a therapist or friends:
"WHAT LIFE TOPICS DO I NEED SPACE
AND TIME TO DEEPLY PONDER?"

_____

_____

_____

_____

_____

_____

_____

_____

_____

_____

their lives. Especially if it is socially validated, for example, getting married or gaining higher education, working for a reputable company, etc. We seek approved forms of the success we aspire to. But what happens when social conventions do not show life paths that include the special details of our own truths?

I suffered deeply because I didn't know anyone else who had gone through a life-changing love that was enduring for years even in that person's absence. For a long time, I didn't know anyone else who was seeing their lover in regular dreams that felt as real as day. Or who felt empty and bored in the company of other romantic interests, like losing your sense of taste. The experience of love I was having did not look like what I had seen for others around me, and so I decided the problem was me. I punished myself. I went in the opposite direction from where the truth of my life was leading me. Dragging myself against the grain. I told myself that as long as I was the only one feeling these things I was wrong, and I interrogated myself over and over on a loop. Every time the light of my truth shone in the darkness of my solitary hermit's path, I put it out. Discarding the wisdom that was buried underneath my judgments was causing me to feel lost and confused; I returned to the starting point of my search for meaning over and over again.

THE TRUTH BELONGS TO YOU

Honoring our truth, even when it is unverified or without social validation, is a way of creating a healthy and adaptable mind. Especially because some things take time and experience to fully understand. Sometimes it is not a matter of being *wrong* but that what we know is *incomplete*. Fielding our thoughts and beliefs to others prematurely is like being given college exams ten minutes into the first day of high school. Why open ourselves to the examination and scrutiny of the beliefs and convictions of others before we have had the time to experience and work through our own? It took me years to understand that I was not wrong just because I was experiencing something different. Instead, those experiences were opening me up to a world beyond what I already knew; and that is a path to wisdom.

There are things you know based on the experiences you have had in life. You know the joys and the challenges of your story. For example, you may have knowledge that comes from being queer or having a disability; growing up somewhere remote; being multilingual; or in my case being a spiritual practitioner. That doesn't mean you have to be a teacher on any of those topics. But taking The Hermit journey can make you a good student. You can learn things that truly matter to you.

Even if you are the kind of person who is generally resolute and unswayed by the strong opinions of others, it does not void the value of Hermit-type introspection and contemplation. The solitude of The Hermit is not beneficial because we are scared of the strong opinions of others, but as a practice of emotional and mental balance. We can connect with others with the stability and trust that come from having committed time, love, and energy to ourselves. Honoring our time as The Hermit deepens our self-awareness. It allows us to be relaxed and open with respect for the other worlds of experience that exist in another person's mind. One of the most courageous things we can do is be honest with ourselves, embracing the knowledge that comes from our emotions and intuition. This can be difficult in a cynical society where everything is expected to be scientifically and rationally legitimized to be trusted. It is difficult because to follow a star (a hope or even astrology), to trust signs and symbols to give us meaning, going against the cultural mainstream, may open us to ridicule.

FINDING MY VOICE

It took me a long time to give myself permission to define my truth on my own terms. When I looked to others for examples there were theories out there about soulmates and spiritual love. But there were also people I respected who criticized, mocked, and renounced theorizing an endless love in that way. Twin Flames (connected souls eternally drawn to one another, compelled to confront internal emotional blocks and circumstantial obstacles on a journey to reuniting) is one of the more popular and most

TAROT THERAPY REFLECTION

Shuffle and pull three tarot cards, or journal
and discuss with a therapist or friends:
"WHAT PERSONAL TRUTHS CAN BE
VALIDATED BY MY OWN LIFE STORY?"

_____

_____

_____

_____

_____

_____

_____

_____

_____

_____

_____

_____

contentious soulmate theories. I read and researched and was conflicted until I stopped to truly hear my own voice.

Finding my own truth and my own voice meant letting go of any and all lies I had been telling myself to try to survive. Throughout those years it was the tarot that helped me to do this. It was in tarot readings that I was reminded of the truth that I was repeatedly running from. It was the tarot that pointed me back in his direction when I was trying to be cold and disconnected. It was the tarot that challenged and rejected the lies I told myself, like "He doesn't care about me," so that I could rip my heart away from the connection after we ended. I don't know that I ever would have given up my mendacity without the tarot as a mirror to my deepest truths. This is the remedy I share with you through Tarot Therapy.

It was through the tarot that I was able to stop *minimizing* the importance of love in my life story. It was not "just a relationship." I wasn't just stuck on a man. When I stopped judging myself I was able to see the meaning for me: he's my family. There were no other teachings of soulmates or star-crossed lovers that described more accurately the bond I have with him besides family. *Not that we are related by blood. But he is kin to my heart and soul.* This perspective was the path to my peace. It gave me space to accept the love I felt but also the distance between us without seeing it as a paradox. Firstly, because being estranged from many of my relatives, I know that family can live very separate lives. Secondly, because he is not the only member of my heart family. There are others who have entered my life over the years and become a part of me—connections that would last forever either by enduring or by the ways they changed me for the better with their love.

The Hermit periods of our life are transient. Pictured with his lantern in the dark landscape traveling through the night, The Hermit has to become ready for the return of daylight: to be seen. It is not enough just to tell ourselves our truth. We also have to live it. We have to find places in the world where we can take up space because finding our voice also involves having others to speak to. Sometimes the night—darkness and secrecy—can protect us. It can give us the privacy we need to risk the first steps of vulnerability. But shame has a way of relegating us to the shadows even in the brightness of day. It can cause us to live in hiding. Seeing others go unapologetically in their own direction, deciding the terms of their own relationships is the gift of the Hermit archetype. In this book I share my stories with you as another step in claiming my wisdom: *overcoming shame*.

For me it was a relationship, but for you it could be something else. An experience you are confused or exasperated by. Something that makes you feel like you won't be accepted. I want to save you time and heartache by telling you that conflict with yourself is the antithesis of the peaceful state of mind that creates room for wisdom. You may have to become The Hermit and walk alone sometimes. Even when you do, don't be the kind of hermit that is split-minded and ranting to themselves down a road of loneliness. Be a friend to yourself by really *listening*. Even if you turn out to be wrong later, you'll be wiser without being unnecessarily wounded by being at war with yourself. I remained on my Hermit path until I learned to see and hold the multiple truths inside me. It also taught me respect for The Hermit journey of others, the space and patience needed for others to also confront their struggles to find truth, and to find the courage to speak honestly.

The Hierophant

Tradition, teacher, law,
counsel, advice, marriage,
test, gatekeeper

The Hierophant tarot card represents tradition and the customs and beliefs we are taught through social institutions and family life. This is one of the major arcana tarot cards that makes the Christian influence very apparent. The Hierophant is pictured as a pope-like figure sitting between two columns with the symbol of two keys at his feet, and disciples bowed low in submission to his wisdom. This card is about religion, belief, and adherence. The teachings of The Hierophant are long-lasting and have resisted the scrutiny of time. In The Hierophant, faith meets practice; it is not enough to only believe. Where the High Priestess is the keeper of spiritual secrets, The Hierophant (High Priest) shares their spiritual knowledge widely. They are who we go to when we can't complete our search for wisdom alone.

The Hierophant is therefore a larger symbol for religious institutions, the education system, the rites of marriage, and more. Contemporarily, we could go as far as to say that news in the form of mass media might also fall under the domain of The Hierophant in the way it directs public opinion. The Hierophant protects and passes down sacred knowledge through generations. With his institutional ties there can sometimes be a tendency to see Hierophant figures as obstructive powers or domineering characters. However, The Hermit path can be dangerous. We can get lost and want to give up, or even find ourselves in difficult situations by following our intuition. In those circumstances The Hierophant can be a necessary guide with wisdom and instruction helping to bring positive change to our lives. They may have long-held methods for healing and wisdom. Jamaican folk medicine and herbalism, for example, is a very sacred tradition that has helped me heal physically and emotionally over the years.

When we don't have an ongoing relationship with a Hierophant figure in the form of a pope, pastor, or priest, we can still benefit from the influence of Hierophant-type moments in our lives. Such as coming across something or someone and hearing exactly what you needed to on that day to give you hope and faith to move forward.

In the symbolism of The Hierophant is a large library of ideas. The Hermit goes to The Hierophant for a wise conversation—what we think and believe from experience in dialogue with what we can be taught or told. The

Hierophant can be an authority figure who examines us as students of life, passing judgment on whether we are succeeding or not. The Hermit's journey is about becoming wise in our own right; shifting the process of judgment to the experienced internal authority of our own hearts and minds. By spending time alone, taking risks to follow our convictions, building an awareness of signs and symbols in the natural world, and gaining life experience by testing our truths, we find the courage to speak back to all the different Hierophant voices in our lives.

Even when being a gatekeeper of knowledge, The Hierophant can act in beneficial ways by protecting the boundaries and integrity of a spiritual and cultural way of life. For example, recently, in part due to celebrities like Beyoncé, orisha (deities of the Ifa religion) have become more mainstream. Priests and initiates of this religion have sought to correct misinformation; Oshun and Yemoja, for example, two of the more popular orisha, are not water goddesses of love and sexuality to be evoked flippantly. Likewise, in my role as spiritual teacher, there have been times when I have cautioned someone that they are not ready to take on a specific spiritual responsibility. Or indicated when they should be honing a spiritual skill or be more mindful of their safety. Having wise and experienced teachers means that we can learn safely under the best possible conditions for our growth.

ARE YOU SURE?

Nevertheless, The Hierophant can be a disruptive figure when there is an abuse of power. Which in spiritual spaces can look like someone attempting to be a proxy for the divine by going beyond reasonable boundaries of influence. Hierophant-type people in our lives can sometimes become punishing and inflexible when their principles are challenged, refusing to consider new insights or the changing circumstances of modern life. For example, right before my GCSEs (secondary school exams) I was kicked out of my English Literature class because a teacher who was new to the school was adamant that I follow his style of exam preparation. During class he would dictate the interpretations of the text that he wanted everyone to write down and memorize. But I had my own thoughts and analysis of Shakespeare and Wilfred Owen and George Orwell. My teachers up until that point had always encouraged my keen insights and creative engagement with the texts. When he challenged me, and I said I had written my own notes, he evicted me from class just weeks before my exams. Ever The Hermit, I studied alone. I took great pleasure on results day, going up to him to say I had not only gotten an A⁺, but full marks on my English Literature exam paper.

There will be times in our lives when a Hierophant figure will undermine our voice and what we know. It can lead to imposter syndrome where we question our right to even be in a space or speak at all. We can be left

TAROT THERAPY REFLECTION

Shuffle and pull three tarot cards, or journal
and discuss with a therapist or friends:
"WHAT INFLUENCE WOULD BENEFIT
ME MOST AT THIS TIME: HERMIT OR
HIEROPHANT?"

_____

_____

_____

_____

_____

_____

_____

_____

_____

_____

_____

asking, do I know enough? How do I prove what I know? I don't have as much expertise, so is what I have to say even valid or needed? In these situations it is important for us to remember that the Hierophants in our lives have been socially validated, and it is up to us, through the journey of The Hermit, to also validate the different ways we have of creating knowledge. This can be through culture, ancestry, intuition, memory or superstition, through feeling and bodily sensation, etc. We can also affirm that we don't always have to immediately know the *how*; the mechanics of how something works. Knowledge creation is a *process*, and there is value in also respecting the limits of our knowledge. It is useful to have curiosity to find out more, but we can also trust ourselves and the process by doing our best with what we currently know.

TAROT THERAPY REFLECTION

Shuffle and pull three tarot cards, or journal
and discuss with a therapist or friends:
"WHAT BELIEFS AND INFLUENCES DO I
NEED TO BECOME FREE OF?"

_____

_____

_____

_____

_____

_____

_____

_____

_____

_____

_____

THE ONLY WAY TO KNOW IS TO DO

Clients who have had religious upbringings often ask me how to overcome the fear they feel about engaging with tarot, and if it is possible for it to coexist with the religious practices they already have. In my experience, the fear of the unknown is only overcome by taking steps into it. I took to tarot like a fish to water, but *my* big obstacle of fear was around connecting with my ancestors. This is an example of when The Hierophant can be an ally. Ancestral veneration (to give respect and reverence to something) is a common tradition in many parts of the world. In Mexico, where I recently visited, there is a yearly Day of the Dead holiday. This day of celebration to connect with loved ones who have died was actually the theme of the award-winning Disney film *Coco*. Regrettably, the customs of ancestral connection from my culture is not something I was taught by my family. I did not know how to properly respect and live harmoniously with ancestral spirits. So I avoided it because I didn't want to get it wrong or endanger myself. Eventually I simply had to learn by experience, figuring it out as I went along. Once I had started, a couple of good books helped me come up with safe practices. I then created a community for ancestral learning and connection so that we could each draw on each other's wisdom and experience. We were rebuilding our lost traditions for ourselves and future generations. This was a Hermit journey in practice.

Choosing when to be The Hermit or to listen to a

Hierophant is about determining the balance between self-inquiry and external instruction. Even as a spiritual practitioner myself, I spent a lot of time questioning and being hesitant about taking on the Hierophant role and being a leader. Eventually, I understood that the energy of The Hermit is one of the strongest influences in my life and that would be my approach to leadership. I would show people what I know and where I've been and how the journey has impacted me; it is why I have written this book. This is how I chose to claim my voice and my wisdom.

Like me, some of you may feel a strong influence of The Hermit archetype in your life. It will be up to you to become comfortable being a *source* of knowledge. A teacher in the form of the Hierophant is not always guaranteed and sometimes that is in your best interest. You may spend a lot of time at the edge of darkness peering over with your lantern and seeing what life itself has to teach you. The extent of influence of The Hierophant as archetypal spiritual teacher—whether you are one or are seeking one—is something we each have to decide on. Our truths are not universally beneficial. What is helpful and applicable to you may not be the same for someone else. Some things that are being widely taught or shared in spiritual circles would be better suited being respected as a singular path of many—The Hermit's journey. In my own practice, I express myself as The Hierophant to a minimal extent. I prefer to learn alongside others in the exploration of the esoteric, hidden, secret, and sacred.

The Fool

*Openness, new beginnings,
lack of experience, risk, innocence,
optimism, faith, trust*

The Fool is a sign of optimistic inexperience. This major arcana card represents new beginnings in life where we are encountering something for the first time. Traditionally pictured standing at the edge of a cliff with a small packed bag and a puppy companion, The Fool recalls the themes of innocence, trust, and lack of burden. It implies that we have not fallen off the cliff edge before. That we are not seasoned enough to know the dangers we might face. Nevertheless, The Fool is in most cases a positive sign, encouragement or a "yes" when we are pulling a card in the tarot. Not knowing what comes next is not a mark against The Fool. It is a freedom that allows room for the unexpected. In stark contrast to the aged Hermit who knows the potential risks of traveling alone along the dark paths of the mind, The Fool is full of youthful exuberance and poised to optimistically leap into the unknown from the ledge of their beliefs. We are acting as The Fool when we bet on ourselves.

Though we generally take The Fool as a symbol of new beginnings, not all beginnings entail a lack of experience. For example, each new day is a new experience. But it may not be so dramatically different from days past that we still feel wonder, optimism, and faith when passing from Monday to Tuesday. As we explored in chapter 4, life can feel very monotonous. So, The Fool is not just about shiny new *things*. In fact, it more often represents a state of mind. When claiming our wisdom, The Fool is how we negotiate between The Hermit (the knowledge we have earned and the lessons that shape us) and The Hierophant (the beliefs that we are taught and the systems of knowledge that challenge and support us). As The Fool we are open to listen, open to try, trusting ourselves to find new and beneficial paths through life.

UNLIKELY CHOICES

The Fool has a unique approach to gathering wisdom, and it comes from their innocence. With age, The Hierophant and The Hermit can tend to feel that they have seen it all before. But The Fool is uniquely placed to find wisdom in the unlikely or seemingly impossible. This is a card about taking risks. Of the three archetypes in this chapter, The Fool is the purest symbol of faith. The Hermit has the benefit of life experience, The Hierophant has the knowledge of the dangerous paths to avoid, but The Fool has only themselves and faith in invisible forces of support. The Fool unlocks important wisdom by being willing to do things others would not. This could be quitting a job without a new income lined up—which at face value would not seem wise at all. Or like my situation, it could be packing up and leaving the country with no plan and no idea of how long I'd be gone. Neither

TAROT THERAPY REFLECTION

Shuffle and pull three tarot cards, or journal
and discuss with a therapist or friends:
"WHAT NEW EXPERIENCES ARE
OPEN TO ME?"

_____

_____

_____

_____

_____

_____

_____

_____

_____

_____

_____

_____

a retreat into solitude (Hermit) nor relying on tradition (Hierophant) can replace the need for risk on the path to becoming wise.

The Fool stands at the cliff's edge of knowledge and wisdom. A symbol for knowing that we can always learn and be shown more. That we are not afraid to fall, that is, to be wrong. The loss of innocence that happens in the coming-of-age process is irreversible (child into adult). So, The Fool is not about being youthful or childlike in age. As the first major arcana card (in some older systems as number 0 it is interchangeable as the first or last card), The Fool has a special relationship to the final major arcana: The World—a symbol of completion. Together like two sides of a door they represent a continuous cycle of life experiences and opportunities for growth.

STARTING OVER

The aspect of new beginnings in The Fool card is not exclusively about first times. In fact, The Fool symbolizes the mindset we need to try again after a setback. When we consider life as a test or lesson, The Fool is a do-over after being marked incomplete by the universe. Like The Fool, none of us soar through life without failure and setbacks. When it comes to major life lessons, we rarely get it the first time; inexperience leads to confusion and mistakes, and we learn from the consequences. We repeat themes and lessons in our lives over and over, sometimes for years, upskilling each time. It is similar to when I

TAROT THERAPY REFLECTION

Shuffle and pull three tarot cards, or journal
and discuss with a therapist or friends:
"WHAT LESSONS AND EXPERIENCES AM I
CURRENTLY REPEATING?"

_____

_____

_____

_____

_____

_____

_____

_____

_____

_____

was seeing a vocal coach because I wanted to get back to the joy I had in singing. My voice was weakened from years of underuse, but there was one session after weeks of practice that I hit a note I did not think I could. It was the most amazing moment of freedom. I had to be willing to go back to singing and learn a totally new approach. The Fool therefore can represent the necessary repetition of the same level, but is also a sign of our continuous novice state whenever we graduate to new levels and opportunities. The perpetual "beginner's mind" is not a condition of misery from being made to repeat. Instead, it is a symbol of hope that there will be another chance to get things right, because sometimes the stakes are much higher than the falsetto I was reaching for in my vocal class. Sometimes our survival or peace relies on us expanding in knowledge and wisdom. We repeat our lessons in life until we become free.

Most people expect their path through life to be a linear progression. A "meritocracy," so to speak—believing you will move from one success to another if you simply apply enough effort. In my experience, the path of wisdom is much more akin to the infinity symbol. We start at the center point, move up in the highs and jubilations of positive experiences, then find ourselves on a descent through losses and failures. It feels like we are moving backward toward the center, our starting point, as we reflect on most recent life lessons. Once we feel centered we continue backward and up as we prepare to try again. We likely have some assistance or an affirming sign that gives us a boost of optimism as a high point in our journey. We feel the momentum of our wisdom gained as we travel down-ward through similar experiences doing things differently, eventually arriving at the center as we travel upward and forward in the rewarding experience of our recent efforts. Now we are ready to experience life at a new level. This pattern of ups and downs repeats. The center point of the infinity symbol is where you'll find the archetype of The Fool, with all the other major arcana cards positioned as experiences along the rising and falling loops. Our wisdom comes through the courage to experience it all.

6

HOPE

Building Your Strength by Exploring Your Anger

Strength, The Sun, Justice

Many of us come to a spiritual experience or tradition desiring a change in some aspect of our lives, and it is exciting when we start to see differences as the result of changed beliefs or new practices we try. Suddenly we have these new ways to create, and it can be so seductive to feel that we can overcome every challenge through the rhetoric of spiritual self-empowerment. To believe that having a positive mindset is enough to keep the unhappiness of life at bay. However, it isn't. Our emphasis on *healing* and *change* in spiritual communities can make it seem like a spiritual path should save us from pain. That if we follow certain steps like a formula we shouldn't have to suffer. But no matter how much more confident and in charge we feel, or how much power we gain from using spiritual tools, it is not guaranteed to us that things in our lives will come quickly or easily. We aren't always in control, and sometimes we are subject to enduring difficult times through no fault of our own.

HOPE AND PATIENCE

Even when it's not the worst of times, there are still occasions when despite our strong will and best efforts a circumstance is not changing. This is why I often joke that *patience* has become like an expletive to me; it is spiritual advice I have been given many more times than I would like. Yet we don't speak openly and frequently enough about how much *waiting* there is on a spiritual path. We focus on change and action and what we can do. But what about the times when we are faced with the limitations of our power? The times, for example, when the change and actions we need are connected to the decisions of others and we have no control over what they will do. Or what about when change takes time? It could require your emotional growth over a period of months. Or be dependent on news and information that hasn't arrived yet. There are times during our spiritual journey when all we can do is take care of present responsibilities and wait. These are my least favorite moments, especially if we're not sure the change we want is even possible. When we are being divinely asked to wait on a very uncertain future, having hope can feel painful as it snags against our real doubts and fears.

Often, our spiritual journey will require us to have hope in something we see or know through our intuition but have no real-world experience of. Or no external proof that what we believe is true. Maybe you are the first in your family to live the way you do or to create something. Or maybe the society you live in has defined what is possible or not, and you feel stifled in trying to do something you've never seen done before. In these moments I often think about the ancestors who were born into slavery. Who in their life experience had only known captivity, but from the wisdom of the spirit—their intuitive vision of freedom—fought for their liberation in a punishing world that said they could be nothing but property, easily replaced and disposed. Change, for them, took centuries.

There are times when we will have to wait for things to happen or develop, but patience doesn't mean being idle. It is about the way we experience the passing of time on the journey to what we hope for. In chapter 5, I talked about not giving myself grace, and the pain I put myself through by fighting against the hope of reconnecting with a soulmate. Those lessons came from all the mistakes I made over the years. This lesson though, this perspective on hope, is the new beginning and The Fool's journey that chapter 5 ends on. It is repeating the cycle of life lessons with more wisdom and experience, choosing to go through it differently this time.

The lesson of patience is to experience the repeated life cycle with less suffering. For example, if I could promise you that something you deeply wanted would definitely happen in exactly one year, how would you live up until that point? Would you be miserable and dejected and disinterested in your life until that date came? Or would you choose to be present and involved with everything happening in the unfolding year, knowing that each day was bringing you closer to your dream? This is what it means to have faith (which steps in as a promise of something better), and to act with hope and patience, even when you have to wait for and believe in a future you can't yet see.

Strength

Will power, self-control,
unbridled emotion, self-belief,
passion, desire, hunger

I have always been enamored with the big cat family, right down to the fact that my name, Leona, means "lion", and so I have a real affinity with the major arcana card Strength. **Associated with the zodiac sign Leo and pictured with a woman dressed in all white, and at ease with her hands on the jaws of a lion, this card is about connecting with our wild nature and the fierceness of our desires. Drawing courage and creative power from within.** The main theme here is *inner strength* as a contrast to the physical strength that we can develop with our bodies. The Strength major arcana card is about the qualities that we cultivate and the development of character to withstand the pressures of life. Similar to the discussion of the subconscious in chapter 2, the lion represents our inner shadow. Not as a beast we have to tame and subdue, but as a source of great passion and power.

TAROT THERAPY REFLECTION

Shuffle and pull three tarot cards, or journal
and discuss with a therapist or friends:
"WHAT PRESENT LIFE SITUATIONS
REQUIRE MY PATIENCE?"

_____

_____

_____

_____

_____

_____

_____

_____

_____

_____

_____

_____

It's easy to say "be strong," but rather than talking to you about squaring your shoulders and enduring through life challenges, I want you to instead think about the Strength card as a symbol for the many raw emotions we have to work with (hands on the open jaws of the lion) through our resilience. The emotions that come up when it gets difficult to be patient or to have hope. When it feels like we are experiencing an injustice in our personal lives (like a colleague lying about you at work), or witnessing it as a dynamic in the wider world (war, racism, destruction of the environment, etc.).

WHEN HOPE STIRS ANGER

I have found in my practice that anger is a very common reaction to tarot messages both in private sessions and in a community setting. Being told to be patient can be infuriating. Being asked to trust can make you want to sneer at the message. But more than anything, being told that something good and worthwhile will eventually come from your efforts when you are struggling and tired and everything seems to be going wrong, well, that can make you want to scream and shout!

Having to be the bigger person, the virtuous one. Always following the guidance and taking the high road. Intuiting things and having to hold those secrets, or speaking up and telling a truth and not being believed. There are times on a spiritual journey when we will feel really hard done by and angry, not just at others around us, but at the divine itself. Times when we ask a higher power, "Why is this happening? Why can't you change it?" Being told to hope through the tarot can bring up feelings of anger because it confirms our fears, that whatever is troubling us is going to continue for the time being; that there is no immediate salvation. Pulling the Strength card in a reading, when you feel you have already been so strong for so long, can feel like a breaking point.

In those times, like the lion on the Strength card with the woman companion who does not fear it, we need to be able to express our anger without being chastised. As a woman, and a Black woman especially, it can be hard to practice this because historically ingrained racial stereotypes mean my anger is perceived in the world as petulant, unseemly, and unjustified. My anger is not socially acceptable. Even for Serena Williams, a Black woman who is one of the most successful and most famous athletes in the world, when she expressed her anger and frustration over a tennis match, she was sanctioned and grotesquely ridiculed in the press. But when men in the sport and her white women counterparts have emoted in the exact same way, they have received empathy and understanding. In fact, for Black people in Europe and America, we know that expressing our legitimate anger can actually put our lives in danger. Most of the time when I am angry I cannot show it without feeling that I am risking everything including my safety, and so it seethes and simmers in the background, scalding me instead.

In other instances, even without the burdens of racial prejudice, for some of you it is the norms of "professionalism" that may curtail your anger. We can't shout in the workplace or tell our line managers exactly what we think. Sometimes we can't even be assertive, from fear that if we are not "likable" anymore, if we don't adopt the dominant corporate culture of public pleasantries and passive aggressive emails, then we are penalized, held back in our jobs, and sometimes sabotaged behind the scenes.

On a more personal level, you may have been on the receiving end of other people's anger expressed as violence or verbal abuse. If you have only ever experienced anger as threatening and destructive, it can bring up a lot of fear and lead to you rejecting your feelings of anger, because you don't want to replicate the harm that was done to you. But having no outlet for our anger disconnects us from our power.

TAROT THERAPY REFLECTION

Shuffle and pull three tarot cards, or journal
and discuss with a therapist or friends:
"IN WHAT AREAS AM I STRUGGLING TO
EXPRESS MY ANGER?"

_____

_____

_____

_____

_____

_____

_____

_____

_____

_____

_____

UNAPOLOGETICALLY ANGRY

When our social norms dissuade us from connecting to our anger, we often don't know how to deal with those feelings when they come up in the context of our spiritual paths. The fear is that our anger cannot always be controlled—but embracing the parts of ourselves that cannot just be pushed into submission is part of the "shadow work" we discussed in chapter 2 through the perspective of The World major arcana card. Anger is like fire. We can use the heat of a flame to cook beautiful meals, but that same flame in a different context could spread and burn a forest to ashes. That anger can be destructive does not mean there is no positive use for it. Destruction is an important part of the creative cycle of life; where one thing ends or changes form and another begins.

Continuing with the symbolism of the lion on the Strength card, though lions are associated with strength and vitality, I've noticed from wildlife documentaries (high five to fellow David Attenborough fans) that there is a public perception of the males being lazy. This is because typically lionesses do all the hunting for the pride, yet the males will eat first and have the largest share of the kill. This seems unfair on the surface, until you understand the purpose of a male lion in a pride: to defend the territory and protect the lives of the lionesses and cubs at the risk of death.

I once watched the most violent lion documentary I have ever seen where, during a clash for territory, a lion had his spine severed and still had to fight to the death while partially paralyzed. After seeing that, I understood. I, too, would rest as much as possible and eat a great deal if my life involved fighting for the protection of my family; having to win that struggle, or otherwise face death or exile from younger and stronger lions. The point here is that sometimes the destructive energy of anger is needed to protect our boundaries. It is not a state that serves us to stay in at all times. Like lions who lounge around and are playful, we need rest, pleasure, and creativity too. But to have that we need to be able to fight and advocate for ourselves. We need our inner fire, and for some of us it does not feel easy or safe to connect to.

The common advice about anger involves "getting rid of it." When I was struggling most with anger about things that were happening to me, I couldn't find examples of how I could *use* my anger. It was all about depleting the power of the anger: "Throw something, break something, get it out of your system, shout!" But that felt futile to me. There weren't enough things I could break or throw to remedy it. There wasn't an exercise program radical enough to evaporate my anger in sweat. What I needed was not to make it into something else or release it. My anger needed direct expression for exactly what it was.

Our anger is not something we should get rid of. Our hope and our anger have to coexist. In fact, sometimes, our feelings of anger will be the thing to energize our hope right at the point that it is failing. It also means, yes, sometimes having a heated argument and even cursing

TAROT THERAPY REFLECTION

Shuffle and pull three tarot cards, or journal
and discuss with a therapist or friends:
"WHAT BOUNDARIES NEED ENFORCING
OR PROTECTING IN MY LIFE?"

_____

_____

_____

_____

_____

_____

_____

_____

_____

_____

_____

people out. Giving fire to our words and our truth can actually burn through obstacles to leave a new path to healing and possibility for change in its wake. We can experience healing and strength when we feel that we have honored and respected ourselves by speaking up and giving true words to the intensity and urgency of our feelings and needs.

Embracing our anger means being willing to be troublesome. To cause an issue. Why should others be at peace at our expense? Sometimes we have to make our problem a shared problem so that others are also motivated toward change. This is the basic premise of going on strike: if my issue is going unanswered, I take strategic action in a way that creates a problem for you, so that now we must negotiate and work together to resolve both.

When I was heartbroken and stuck in pain for years, it was my anger that I expressed by creating drama that brought change. No amount of tears, or periods of endurance, patience, understanding, clear communication, or hope was changing anything. My rage was the catalyst for my freedom. My anger was what made me say I don't accept this, and I am going to *create* a change. My anger made me handle the situation differently than how I normally would. To act out of my character, even, to embrace my shadow, and in doing that a cycle of suffering in my life crashed and ended.

Our anger is a powerful communication tool that we need to give voice and action to. We can use the tarot to hear its words when we feel like it runs too hot to decipher. When it is so primal we need symbols and metaphors before we can find the right expression for it. Our anger can be so impactful in revealing the truth about what we want and the kind of world we want to live in. Especially when pain or hopelessness make us want to disconnect and give up on our desires. The lion on the Strength card reminds us that our passion and desire are connected to our anger, and if we discard our anger we also lose strength and creativity. We give up some of our life force.

SUPPRESSING ANGER, LOSING HOPE

At times, we may be angry at people or events where we can't safely actualize our anger. We may find that there is someone we hold *responsible* for a problem, but we don't have the power or community to hold them *accountable*. Often our anger manifests as a reaction to feeling powerless, and our unexpressed anger turns into resentment. Where anger can be energizing, opening us to new levels of personal strength and resolve, resentment is instead like having our potential in a corroding battery. When we are resentful we don't use the power of our anger. Instead it is a process of embitterment that is like being slowly poisoned by our own emotional pain. Instead of taking direct action with courage, when we are bitter our anger seeps out. It is acidic. It doesn't have the diversity of our inner fire that can be expressed as passion or joy as well as anger.

Our bitterness is like toxic waste. It festers in our silence and the only way to recover is to bring our pain

TAROT THERAPY REFLECTION

Shuffle and pull three tarot cards, or journal
and discuss with a therapist or friends:
"WHAT DO I FEAR ABOUT EXPRESSING
MY ANGER?"

_____

_____

_____

_____

_____

_____

_____

_____

_____

_____

_____

_____

back out into the light of day. To expose it with truth. Healing means making our feelings of powerlessness known to people we are safe with. It means the possibility of finding collective power by sharing our struggles with others because we can't overcome everything alone. In our isolation, resentment becomes feelings of futility. Our sense of things being futile is a retreat space where we decide to accept our powerlessness. Where our belief is "nothing good will come of this, so I won't try."

When we don't express our anger, we move further and further away from hope. Hopelessness is having no expectation of a positive outcome. But futility is a refusal to recognize our role in bringing about change. When we feel everything is futile, we act in protest. It is a resistant state where we refuse to engage, and that takes energy for us to maintain. It doesn't serve us, however, to use our energy toward keeping ourselves stuck.

Repressing and rejecting our anger is a path to abandoning hope. Our creativity and survival in this world are dependent on our ability to see more than the immediate moment. To have hope that what comes next could be different from the life events that have already gone. The lion's companion on the Strength card reminds us that expressing our anger is cleansing. As she stands next to the lion, the symbolism of her white attire is a message that being connected to our anger as an inner fire is purifying. It metabolizes our pain and gives us purpose through our difficulties. Engaging with our anger with honesty can bring clarity of perspective. To trust our anger, to make use of it, is to move with power even if in small ways. The embers of our anger are enough to rekindle our hope. Showing us that we are reflections of nature and, just like the catalyzing power of fire, our anger is the same elemental force, our own tool for change.

The Sun

Growth, blessing, joy,
clarity, optimism, childhood

While there are no "bad" tarot cards (even Death and The Devil are constructive), there are some cards that when you see them, you know they will signify something difficult that has to be confronted. **The Sun card is on the opposite of this. It's one of those cards that clients immediately smile about and let out a little sigh of relief. It is generally a positive omen. It is illustrated as a joyful scene with a naked child riding a white horse and waving a red flag against the backdrop of a huge sun in the sky and a garden full of sunflowers. This is a good time! The Sun card represents happy conclusions or joyful new beginnings. It is about innocence and freedom and play. It is about experiencing the brighter side of life and being supported in our creativity and dreams.** The Sun card symbolizes feeling blessed. It is having our hope rewarded through the fruition of our dreams.

The beautiful experiences encapsulated in the themes of The Sun card are what we hope for. While it represents the end goal—the sun as the source of life on Earth—it also represents how we feed our hopes. How we use our sun-filled visions and dreams to renew our strength and courage. Often these visions and hopes will return to us again and again through our intuition, in dreams, in tarot readings. Perhaps through signs and serendipity in the outer world. If you have ever tried, you will know it can be very difficult to stamp out our hopes. Even when we commit to gloom and hopelessness, our hearts say otherwise. The love we feel—for ourselves, our communities, our environment, our allied spirits, and the divine—is limitless and it is always showing us that the bleakness we feel now can be replaced with light. The Sun card is then about the renewal of hope, just as the sunrise is a promise that follows its evening descent.

The Sun card also shows us the abundance of creative routes for our anger to go when our fight is no longer required and beautiful moments in our lives have finally arrived. The image of the naked toddler on The Sun card is about being open to the new dawn (a positive change or outcome). Children, for example, move through emotional states very quickly. From anger and frustration to laughter, or from exhilarated to tired and ready for a nap. The child riding on the horse represents being able to let go of the heavy burdens of the past and to be uplifted by our blessings.

The lightheartedness of The Sun card is an important message because sometimes, especially when we have persevered through long challenges, even though a circumstance improves we may not feel ready to adjust emotionally to the change. An apology from someone and an attempt to right a wrong or reconcile with us does not

TAROT THERAPY REFLECTION

Shuffle and pull three tarot cards, or journal
and discuss with a therapist or friends:
"WHAT IS MY HEART ASKING ME
TO HAVE HOPE IN?"

_____

_____

_____

_____

_____

_____

_____

_____

_____

_____

_____

mean that our many feelings about the situation, especially our anger, suddenly disappear. We may find that we are unexpectedly attached to our grief, or resentment, or futility, because they played a protective role for us. We may feel that those emotions guarded us from being exposed to further hurt from others and it is not an armor we feel safe to do without. The Sun card asks us to bring our fears of the dark nights in our lives into the brightness of the day. To experience another kind of protection through practicing truth, honesty, and vulnerability.

In the blessed seasons of lives, our anger becomes art. If we do not suppress and deny our anger in times of hardship, that wisdom remains when things are well. When life is good, especially when it has become so through the power and catalyst of expressing anger, this is a time to honor our inner fire. One of the ways this is done is through body art, color, piercings, and tattoos, etc.—outwardly marking the life change and stories we have lived through. "Makeup" sex is another popular trope as the expression of anger, pain, and hurt during a relationship reconciliation and the recovery of loving feelings. It is acknowledging the *anger* with the *hope* for the relationship. This puts into practice the power of anger and hope coexisting, an idea we discussed earlier in this chapter.

We may want to give voice to our anger through our creative works weaving in the wisdom we have gained along the way to make something beautiful of our struggles. This book is also part of the legacy of my anger. In it I have directed the power of so many moments of being angry and feeling mistreated into hopeful words.

Through the symbolic creative outlet of The Sun card we can allow our anger to rest through choices we make, like forgiveness or trust. The opening of our hearts is what it means to be lighthearted; to not be weighed down and blocked by fear and trauma. By not dismissing our anger when we are opening our hearts to life and to people, we allow the inner fire of anger to become a sentinel. That is, a guard and watcher. Like the lion who rests whenever he is not being challenged to fight, and enjoys his bonds of kinship with his pride; who patrols the borders of his territory daily to keep everyone protected. We can also allow our anger to settle into peace. Knowing that it is a strength available to us if our boundaries are challenged in the future.

Justice

Balance, consequence, correction,
responsibility, futurism, spiritual laws

It is very confronting to write about justice from a spiritual perspective, when there is so much social unrest and injustice in the world. Even more so if we imagine justice to come through some form of divine intervention where a higher power makes things right on our behalf. The briefest world history shows us this is not the case. That for centuries people have prayed and petitioned and asked for help but the wickedness and greed in the world has persisted. My Bible knowledge has become patchy since I stopped going to church, but there are always a few lines that stay with me. Like when King David says in the psalms that when he saw that wicked people prospered in life, he almost fell over. I love this because it is so relatable to the shock and bemusement we feel when our integrity and virtue seem not to count.

The Justice card in the tarot is pictured as a person seated between two pillars in front of a red veil, wearing a red robe, and with a sword raised in one hand and scales held in the other. This card is associated with the zodiac sign Libra. In some of the newer indie decks, Justice is illustrated as a person holding the sword and scales but blindfolded; and I think this seeks to reflect the contemporary mood around the injustice in the world. The meaning of the Justice card is to bring balance and fairness through judgment and consequence. It is about weighing actions and testimonies to decide on a truth. This is not the kind of personal truth we have thus far discussed in this book. The role of justice is to judge the truth according to "spiritual law" and to hold individuals accountable to the consequences of their actions, and any corrections they may need to make.

Spiritual law doesn't necessarily mean religious law or principle. It is about the way we observe the spiritual dimension of life interacting with the physical. Therefore, justice is not the verdict of a single person but the feedback or consequences that are triggered by our choices. For example, the law of attraction is one that has become mainstream. It states that what we focus on (giving our time, energy, and attention to) is what we draw more of into our lives. This law is frequently misrepresented by the hyper-materialism of this era where people expect it to work like a wish list. That is, if I say that I want a million-dollar house I should get it because I am attracting and "manifesting" it. This law does not, however, mean you get whatever you wish for. It means you get more of what you invest in—not specifically with money but with your energy. There isn't a literal judge who descends from the heavens to check what you are focusing on. Justice unfolds as your experience. For example, it makes me think of popular gossip bloggers who decide to completely shift their brand because constantly promoting and engaging with negative stories started to diminish their well-being and quality of life.

We can become jaded, angry, and hopeless when we are expecting our lives to change through the miracle of divine intervention. I don't mean to suggest that there is no higher influence in our day-to-day, but that *we* are the divine intervention we are looking for. That the creation of justice as a divine principle and spiritual law is through our actions. Like the biblical story of King David—dismayed at the injustice he saw, he was also afforded power and influence to create the just world he believed in. Sometimes we are waiting for salvation that will only come through us. Or we are the person well placed to do something that will create justice for someone else. But we are waiting on the divine. There is wisdom in knowing when to refrain from doing something as you allow other factors and roles to take shape, and when it is your time on the stage of life to contribute your unique gifts and perspective.

There is a separation between the physical dimension

TAROT THERAPY REFLECTION

Shuffle and pull three tarot cards, or journal
and discuss with a therapist or friends:
"IN WHAT AREAS OF LIFE AM I EXPECTING
TO BE RESCUED BY SOMEONE ELSE?"

_____

_____

_____

_____

_____

_____

_____

_____

_____

_____

_____

_____

and the spiritual one; otherwise we wouldn't need intuition or methods of divination. We wouldn't need our faith; everything would be very clear and plain to see. In the separation of dimensions, we use the spiritual tools we have to support us in our journeys through life. Sometimes that means activating our anger in a practical way and speaking up, being the divine influence right here, right now. Sometimes it is using tarot to come up with a plan for how to advocate for ourselves and others, whether in the workplace or within families. Or taking our anger and grief to our altars and asking for assistance. Working with the elements of the natural world through ritual (using plants and herbs or water from rivers, etc.) to create shifts in energy that can help to change circumstances toward our favor.

There is a common saying in spiritual circles that "what's for you can't miss you," and I have always struggled to see the merit in it. In reality, I find that our blessings and dreams can be delayed, blocked, and obstructed. That the spiritual path is not a passive one and sometimes we have to fight for what we want or the justice that we believe is ours. That we need our anger and strength to face opposition, and that sometimes it comes in unexpected forms. Not just from people but in noticing resistance in energy, such as feeling like you are always swimming against the tide or having to climb uphill. The scales on the Justice card represent us exploring spiritual laws to see the balance between the things that are a consequence of our own actions (which we must take responsibility for and work to resolve where possible), and the things that are incursions from the actions and intentions of other people and influences (that we will have to demand justice for).

In this context, having hope doesn't mean being happy or even optimistic. We can be hopeful and sad, hopeful and worried, hopeful and angry. In whatever combination, our hope is needed because it is the difference between whether we keep creating change, healing, and justice in our lives or resign ourselves to our suffering until the event that something or someone else changes. No matter how restricted we feel, hope is a choice we can make. Hope is our power of change.

THE MODERN WORLD OF TAROT

7

INTUITION

Navigating the Classic Art of Tarot
in the Modern World

Judgment, The Devil, Temperance

Throughout this book I have discussed the tarot as a very personal tool for working through complex and important life issues. I have shown you the ways that I have used tarot in my life, and given you points of reflection to create similar opportunities of healing for yourself. As a tarot therapist, I find it also important to reflect on the growing tarot industry online, including changes to the public perception of tarot, and where our current habits of tarot engagement might possibly lead us. This is an important conversation for tarot readers, as more and more people create businesses and services using the tarot. I'm also passionate that people on the receiving end of tarot content (tarot listeners, clients, the general audience for tarot) are well equipped and supported to engage with this practice in a healthy and edifying way.

If you are completely new to tarot, there may be styles and approaches I refer to that won't be familiar to you yet. Those parts of this chapter will be helpful to people with some experience of giving, watching, or receiving a tarot reading. Nevertheless, there is much said here about the world of tarot that you will find interesting and affirming, even if this is a new topic of exploration for you. If you do use the tarot, some of the critiques I offer may at times feel confronting to read or challenge your current practice. My purpose is not to offend or shock. I am not claiming to know what is best for all people at all times. As someone with a very strong Mercurial Virgo influence, my motivation is to critique for the purpose of improvement (if you have any Virgos in your life then you've experienced this firsthand). I love working with the tarot, perhaps more than any other kind of work I do in my life. Reflecting on the tarot industry is my sign of respect for this long tradition and those of us involved with it.

Judgment

Awakening, divine contact, realization,
verdict, life review, wake-up call

The major arcana card Judgment has come to be one of my favorites in the tarot. The Judgment card is about those sacred moments when we encounter something bigger than ourselves. The bodies rising from coffins in The Judgment card imply rapture: that is, to be drawn up into something transcendent. I have had many of these moments in my life—times when I have felt the love, presence, and support of the divine. Judgment is an experience of spiritual *contact*—it can be a sense or feeling, not having to be specifically words or speech.

In my own practice, when the Judgment card comes up, it can represent the presence and intervention of the many kinds of spirit speakers who show up in our nonphysical environment (ancestors, angels, etc.). I always imagine the scene of the angel blowing the trumpet on the Judgment card as very loud. This is a tarot card about getting our attention. It is the noisiness of this card that also makes me think of the tarot content space as a loud and a bustling spiritual crowd or marketplace. Each tarot reader is blowing their metaphorical Judgment trumpet when giving us a message.

Many tarot readers describe themselves as channeling. That is, the act of directly connecting with spirits and relaying in words what is being shared with them. Creating a transcendent moment of divine contact. This is quite different to the role of The Hierophant, who instructs based on spiritual knowledge developed over time. The Hierophant, even if they consider the divine to be the source of their knowledge, rarely claims to be translating words from God live and direct. But as tarot readers we do this all the time. To open ourselves and others to this practice of divine Judgment is a huge responsibility.

I remember the first time I paid for a tarot reading. It was from a woman on Instagram who I had been following for a while and she had low-cost options for a tarot reading sent by email. I was going through a very difficult time and so I decided to give her a try. It was one of the worst tarot experiences I have ever had. If I were not more resilient it may have altered my life trajectory and turned me off the tarot altogether. Her message was critical, disempowering, and pessimistic. I remember being immediately thrown into dismay, full of fear and doubt about my future. But even then, at the early stages of this journey, my spirit was strong. The next day I felt my intuition and subconscious pushing against her guidance. I could feel deep within me that her words were not true of my life. I realized that the day before I had given a complete stranger so much power over me, and what had I done to discern that she—or anyone—was worthy of that influence?

When I began to read the tarot for others that awful experience was a defining factor in my practice. My ethos is to check the well-being of my clients at the end of a session—even if that means giving them more of my time. When people come to me vulnerable, wanting to place their future in my hands, my principal goal is to keep a boundary against that responsibility, gently reminding them to hold on to their own power, intuition, and decision-making. Even if they've not yet realized it is something they should protect.

Tarot readings that don't connect or are, at worst, detrimental to the well-being of others are one of the reasons "take what resonates" has become a necessary disclaimer from tarot readers. Particularly when the tarot messages are given for the general public. But how do listeners develop the skill of *resonance*? In spiritual communities, resonance refers to the message being harmonious with an existing internal sense of knowing. It requires an activated intuition; and for the general public this is often not the case. The Judgment card is also therefore about prudence in our experiences of spiritual contact and discernment about the spiritual speakers we engage with.

TAROT AND MENTAL HEALTH

As tarot has become mainstream as a growth sector on social media, I have become concerned about the impact of the loud marketplace nature of tarot content today. This is not an attempt to be a gatekeeper, because it will never be up to me to decide who is called to do this work or not. I can have likes and dislikes of tarot styles and readers, but this is not a matter of personality or preferences. As someone passionate about the use of tarot as a therapeutic tool, I am most concerned about the mental and emotional health implications of the mass consumption of tarot messages.

Tarot content online overlaps with the coach and advice sector, and is now commonly used as motivational messages for wide audiences. When it is not specifically used as a method for spiritual guidance and instruction, how do the healing possibilities of tarot change when the advice being shared could be applied to anyone at any given point in time? "Aries, you need to trust yourself," for example, is a positive and motivating message for Aries Sun sign people. But it does not *reveal* the causes of doubt or offer any *spiritual insight* on how to cultivate trust

TAROT THERAPY REFLECTION

Shuffle and pull three tarot cards, or journal
and discuss with a therapist or friends:
"HOW CAN I TEST AND CONFIRM THE
INSIGHTS I GAIN FROM TAROT?"

_____

_____

_____

_____

_____

_____

_____

_____

_____

_____

_____

_____

_____

within ourselves. Aries Sun sign people do need to learn to trust themselves, but of course so does everyone.

For you, the public motivational approach to tarot may be a beneficial practical adaptation to modern times, offering collective inspiration. This might be all that you want from a tarot reading for a wide audience, and that is valid. But in this approach we miss the opportunity to do very necessary healing work in a society that is chronically exhausted, anxious, and depressed. When tarot is separated from its mysticism and esoteric origins we lose our awareness of it as a divination practice; as a tool for higher and wiser judgment. I regularly marvel at the spiritual wisdom the tarot puts me in touch with. I frequently say to my Tarot Therapy community, for example, "Wow, I would never say this or come up with this myself." Like the announcement of the angel in the Judgment card, when I am reading the tarot I am often sharing ideas that are beyond me.

Furthermore, when we remove spirituality from tarot it can become a ventriloquist's doll where tarot messages are really a cover for the inner thoughts of the reader without them clearly stating so. That is, are we using the "good advice" of tarot messages as a subtext or indirect message to someone else we have a problem with? How can the tarot not be the inner thoughts of the reader, you ask? Well, when I begin a tarot reading—whether for an individual or community—I have no idea what message will come through the cards. I don't have an opinion on an issue that I use the cards to demonstrate. I may share my personal opinion or experience during a tarot reading, but I distinguish it as my own thoughts so that listeners can weigh my words appropriately.

TOO MUCH TAROT?

With thousands of tarot readings uploaded to social media every day, where is all this advice leading us? Even as a tarot reader myself I feel the pressure of the constant stream of tarot advice when I am browsing online. Though I make a conscious effort to bypass most of it and only intentionally engage with specific readers that I discern are helpful to me, it is impossible to avoid it all. If we are interested in tarot content, then the social media algorithms give us lots of it. As we scroll the timeline we are ingesting tarot messages whether we want them at that time or not, and it is having an effect.

Mass motivational message tarot and the overabundance of tarot messaging are perhaps most relevant on Twitter, YouTube, and TikTok. On these sites the content feed is curated by the user to a limited extent, and is made up of algorithm-based suggestions to a significant degree. I've noticed that if I like one tarot reading, then my news feed becomes awash with tarot readers. It is like walking down a street after a beautiful and satisfying meal and being repeatedly accosted to enter other restaurants. It's unwanted attention. If we are repeatedly watching or reading all the tarot we see for our zodiac signs, or all the relationship advice in tarot videos with titles that look relevant, then it

TAROT THERAPY REFLECTION

Shuffle and pull three tarot cards, or journal
and discuss with a therapist or friends:
"IS MY CURRENT RELATIONSHIP WITH
TAROT HEALTHY FOR MY MIND?"

_____

_____

_____

_____

_____

_____

_____

_____

_____

_____

_____

_____

is like going into several of those restaurants and eating one full meal after another, making us sick. It is a practice of bingeing, and it is just as unhealthy for our minds as it would be to our bodies. Too much tarot, whether it's our choice to engage or through the push of the industry, compromises our mental health. It can create confusion, anxiety, and mental overwhelm.

Even when tarot messages online aren't negative or damning, they often make suggestions about the kind of day or experiences we could be having, for example. While we can choose to ignore them, our brains are primed for suggestion. Even when we consciously reject messages, we know from all the studies on how mass media and advertising affect us that those messages are programming the subconscious. Where before we may have gone to a specific spiritualist in our community for advice and counsel and built relationships with them—be it a conjure woman or a pastor—we are now the people in the Judgment card in a sea of spiritual advice being pulled in so many directions.

Some of the most popular tarot content is relationship advice, and this makes sense as we all want experiences of love, intimacy, and connection. Many people seek out tarot messages because of experiences of heartbreak, rejection, or loneliness. They are looking for hope. But how can we discern that a given tarot reader has the skill and capacity for advising on healthy and expansive visions for love, partnership, and connection? How often are "general love readings" (perhaps unwittingly) feeding our bad habits, attachments, patterns of avoidance, and demands to have and see things our own way through confirmation bias (that is, using tarot to validate what we already think)? This is one of the ways that general tarot advice is not necessarily helpful, but potentially harmful. In the Judgment card we see the themes of verdict, realizations, and wake-up calls. It is divine intervention for review in retrospect. That is, unfortunately sometimes we only learn the discernment of the Judgment card when we have been wronged or harmed by something. In this case, when our lives start to show the consequences of being ill-advised.

What happens when we come across "general" tarot advice that is not necessarily bad, but is challenging, triggering, or upsetting in some way? For example, a message that warns about an upcoming loss of finances. Or a reading that suggests betrayal from someone close. Good judgment is not just discerning right from wrong, but knowing how to work with the information we have been given. The nature of public tarot readings means there is often no established outlet to work through difficult messages. No personal relationship with the reader to get further clarity on what they meant; or to be supported in processing our feelings about what we have heard. You would be much more likely to be blocked rather than supported if you had any feedback or critique online. Or simply told if the message doesn't resonate, let it go and move on. In addition, we cannot overlook the toxic, entitled, and dependent nature of some tarot audiences and internet trolls that lead tarot readers to turning off replies and comments to protect their own mental health. The more mainstream tarot becomes, especially on the internet, the more important it is that we observe the industry that develops around it so that we can have an impact on the practice, particularly creating healthy boundaries for tarot readers and users, as the dynamics of one-on-one tarot become too narrow to consider the needs of public audiences.

The Devil

Bondage, materialism, deception,
fear, illusion, dead end,
desire, temptation, matrix

Tarot exists now as a growing industry. The opportunity and interest in someone like me to write a book on tarot, without existing ties or professional connections to major publishing houses, would not have been present years ago. There have been many tarot books that are instructional (i.e. this card means this) and many that are theoretical and mystical through a deep dive into tarot symbolism. There are also tarot books that focus on specific issues, such as interpreting readings on love and sex. However, tarot writing solely as an examination of social life is an emerging subject. *Tarot Therapy* is an even newer and growing perspective.

Recognizing the industry means we need to think carefully about our role within it. **This is the significance of the Devil card. It represents materialism and the structures of the physical world. Illustrated as a couple chained to a monstrous figure, it asks us what we are in bondage to. What** are the harmful things that come along with the choices we make and attachments we have? The Devil as antagonist plays a useful role in animating the trappings of life so that we can understand what we need to become free.

THE TEMPTING APPEAL OF TAROT

One of the trappings of the tarot content space at the moment is the *temptation* of possible wealth and fame. Not everybody practicing tarot online is ethical or has honest intentions. Most recently, I saw complaints on Twitter with screenshots of a reader who was sending the exact same messages to multiple clients who had paid them for a tarot reading. There are countless fraudulent readers who have ulterior motives and are driven by the perception that tarot is an easy way to make money fast. Sometimes it is a gateway to other things they would like to do with their fame. So they begin with tarot and then pivot to a different role. That is not to say that if you start tarot you can't stop or change what you do. This is about an intentional exploitation of a community for personal gain; the negative aspect of the materialism of the Devil card. Hungry for celebrity status, these individuals are not doing any of the personal healing or spiritual growth work that would give them the integrity needed in this space.

Even when it is not specifically a dishonest reader, tarot listeners are increasingly being targeted online by scams. A very common issue is fake social media accounts pretending to be popular tarot readers. These readers solicit tarot listeners in comments and direct messages by posing as a tarot reader they follow, and offer a special message in exchange for money. Tarot and spirituality are not immune to imposters. Where the Devil card asks what are the harmful things that come along with our choices, these scams are part of the online safety issue that comes along with tarot in the public sphere.

THE LIMITATIONS OF SOCIAL MEDIA

Tarot in mass media is not inherently wrong, but like the chains on the Devil card it can be tied to things it needs freeing from. What is the role of Twitter, Instagram, TikTok, and YouTube in tarot practice? It can, for example, be an important means of connecting us with like-minded "soul family" and people we are well placed to create a community with. It can be a space where we can locate trusted spiritual advisers and teachers that might otherwise be hard to come by in our day-to-day lives. These platforms also give us access to many communities rather than just one school of thought or one church or temple that we remain in for years. We can have multiple communities of belonging online, and move between them as we grow and change, doing so without drama and judgment. I know from my own experience that people come and go from my community according to their own needs. Some people have been with me for years, while others take time away because their families have expanded, for example. Some members have spent time growing in other spaces and come back months later for the specific blessing and value of the House of Black community. This is healthy and independent growth, and the options and variety are a feature of doing tarot practice online. Being in an online community removes the resource limitations (material restriction being a theme of the Devil card) of having to own or rent physical buildings to gather. One of the major benefits of social media and the online tarot community is that I have been able to travel and lead House of Black from places all over the world.

We can, however, be overzealous about the merits of social media for spiritual work. There are genuine limitations for spiritual community-building that we should think seriously about. This includes, for example, "shadow banning"and being penalized by algorithms for sharing tarot and other esoteric content, which undermines organic community-building. When platforms shadow-ban users, they suppress their visibility and engagement so that their usual audience does not see their content, but without informing the user. The intention is for it to be almost unnoticeable. For example, posting links to your e-commerce site is another action that users have complained has resulted in shadow banning, because the platforms would prefer you to pay for advertising and promoted posts. In this way, suppressing spiritual content represents the Devil card and the commercial greed of huge social media companies as a priority over the value and benefits of spiritual content for community healing and education.

TAROT THERAPY REFLECTION

Shuffle and pull three tarot cards, or journal
and discuss with a therapist or friends:
"WHAT KIND OF SPIRITUAL COMMUNITY
DO I WANT TO BE IN?"

_____

_____

_____

_____

_____

_____

_____

_____

_____

_____

_____

This is also evidence that fear and stigma around some spiritual practices continues in the mainstream.

How do we reconcile the suppression of spiritual content with the simultaneous overconsumption of it on social media? The answer is in the kind of content that is popular, boosted, and financially rewarded. The algorithms that drive social media sites are not accounting for the skill and sincerity of a reader. That is not to say that popular tarot readers are not genuine and very good at what they do. It is more a statement about the conditions for success that often reflect the trappings of the Devil card. For example, is a reader conventionally beautiful? This affects their popularity and success online (as a theme of the Devil card this would be considered *glamor*: the charm or appeal of beauty). Or as a reader, do you feed the algorithm, like the beast of the Devil card, with constant content to stay relevant? Sometimes even at the expense of your health and well-being?

The demand for frequent tarot messages, either as a consequence of having a large audience, or in trying not to be lost in the sea of content, is one of the challenges and concerns of tarot work online. The negative archetypal Devil influence here is the addictive over-reliance of tarot audiences and the bondage of readers to unhealthy or unsustainable rates of creation. What is the motivation for sharing tarot videos and messages several times a day, every day, before a listener has had time to act upon the messages or even experience the unfolding of the tarot advice that happens with time?

I'm certainly not specifically against daily tarot or

spiritual content. Some people do this very well. There are periods of life when I do morning tarot readings for myself daily, so I see the value of it. But there is an emotional and mental cost difference between readings we do for ourselves and how we share our spiritual gifts with the public. If we are engaged in creating tarot content at a *very high volume*, where is the space to practice our own maintenance, serve ourselves, and complete the activities that define our spiritual well-being? We don't want to end up with a spiritual practice but no personal spiritual journey of our own. It is not for me to determine how much tarot content is too much, especially because the answer to that can change depending on other things happening in our lives. But we should each ask ourselves the question and have an answer we are at peace with.

WORKING TO SURVIVE

It is undeniable that contemporary tarot practice is being shaped by our genuine survival needs under capitalism. This is a time of e-commerce where people who have been underemployed or excluded from education and career opportunities are now able to use social media as an avenue to earn an income. As spiritual practitioners we have been able to use our gifts to support our communities *and* make a living.

This is positive and liberating, and I have experienced it in my own practice. But it isn't without the risks of the Devil card's trappings. The challenge is that two things can

TAROT THERAPY REFLECTION

Shuffle and pull three tarot cards, or journal
and discuss with a therapist or friends:
"AM I SERVING MYSELF JUST AS WELL AS
I AM GIVING SUPPORT TO OTHERS?"

_____

_____

_____

_____

_____

_____

_____

_____

_____

_____

_____

happen: **Our survival needs (paying bills, etc.) can over-power the rhythm required to maintain a healthy relationship with our gifts.** That is, capitalism distorts the practice. We may work too-long hours or see too many clients in a given time period. I have definitely been guilty of this in the past. The consequences can be very serious as we deplete both physical and spiritual energy, leaving us more susceptible to health issues if we don't regularly cleanse, protect, and restore our energy. If money is the tie, in the form of the Devil card, to the way we structure our tarot content, then we can't fully experience the creative freedom of this role as a messenger. Through no fault of our own, we simply do not have enough agency. Which leads to the question: can your tarot practice actually support your material needs? As a role lived in service to others it is possible it cannot. Not because you're not good enough, but perhaps it's not your purpose to make a living from tarot. You may be guided to use it in the service of others more intermittently, or just for friends. Or you may have other life challenges (your health or family obligations) that often get in the way of you building a sustainable tarot practice. It is okay if you realize your use of tarot is not going to make a business.

The second challenge is that using tarot to sustain our income can cause people to move too quickly from student to practitioner. Who defines what is too fast? You could ask yourself if money or financial stress were removed as factors in the decision, would a different timeline of practice and experience unfold? Personally, I was reading cards for others within months of learning, and this was very important in developing my craft. But it was years before I had the responsibility of leading a tarot community, and even that was built on a decade of experience in leadership and community-building.

When we don't have adequate time to practice and gain skill—however long that is for each individual—we can make avoidable mistakes and cause harm to ourselves or others. There is no shame in being a novice (like the Fool card and the Page characters in the tarot deck). However, if we don't respect our inexperience, we can end up taking on too much responsibility and not building a solid foundation to define the healthy principles of our practice.

It is valuable to see longevity in the tarot and spiritual wellness space; to be able to see the paths others have developed along and see moments of spiritual initiation in their lives; to learn from their experience and grapple with our own; to see methods and beliefs that have been tested over time; to have the room to gain an understanding of the historical and cultural influences of the things that we practice, avoiding the New Age melting pot that weakens the potency of spiritual traditions by disconnecting them from their culture and theological/theoretical ecosystem—the popularized chakra system is a good example of this, as most people learn about them as points of energy in the body but know nothing of their origin and context in the Hindu belief system. Or another example is, why do people do intention-setting and rituals around moon transits, beyond the prompts of social media infographics? The way that we consume counsel on social media means that we often take for granted what

TAROT THERAPY REFLECTION

Shuffle and pull three tarot cards, or journal
and discuss with a therapist or friends:
"WHAT ARE SOME OF MY PITFALLS OR
BAD HABITS WHEN LISTENING TO
OR INTERPRETING TAROT?"

_____

_____

_____

_____

_____

_____

_____

_____

_____

_____

_____

_____

we are told. We don't benefit from the rootedness and training that come from fully engaging in the spiritual traditions that we are practicing different elements from.

It's important that we don't avoid the work it takes to cultivate a spiritual practice. Otherwise, under pressure of the industry, we will become tarot influencers in materialist and illusory ways. The Devil card in this sense refers to seduction and temptation. However we choose to share and enjoy our work (for example, I love playing with colors and aesthetics in my tarot work), there should be a genuine well-developed practice that underpins everything. This is the positive aspect of The Devil archetype—being challenged into competence and readiness. Finding self-empowerment through resisting the pitfalls and temptations of The Devil and creating an honest, ethical, and honorable relationship to our work.

Temperance

*Alchemy, balance, calm,
measure, practice, study,
guidance, recovery*

The themes of the Temperance card are alchemy, balance, and measure. Temperance is about the experimentation we do to find out what actually works. This is how we learn the correct measure of things; by taking our truth and wisdom from the theoretical to the practical. The message of the Temperance card is to avoid extremes—to temper one's thoughts and actions. It asks us to be measured and to employ checks and balances. Illustrated with an angelic figure pouring from one cup to another, one foot on the water and the other on the land, this card symbolizes restoring the balance through healing and renewal. It is the practice of being tended to. In the Temperance card we learn the value of being able to soothe and calm. To give ourselves and others time, room, and space.

Following the discussion on the tarot industry and its challenges, the medicine of the Temperance card is not to take all that I have said to denigrate other perspectives and practices. Neither is it to defensively cling to what we already think and do and reject the legitimate questions posed in this chapter. Instead it is to try a measure of things. To see what combinations of wisdom and practice create the intended results for you. Using the archetypal wisdom of the Temperance card, I'd like to share some thoughts I have about the possibilities for positive tarot practices and the healing power of tarot when practiced in community.

PRACTICING TAROT ONLINE

There is so much healing, boundary, and support work needed around tarot practice as it becomes more and more mainstream. How can tarot readers, like myself, help to educate tarot audiences so that they are empowered and well prepared to engage the tarot constructively? One of the ways we can do this is by more clearly defining who a tarot message is for and who we intend to speak to rather than just labeling all public tarot as a "general reading." When we have clear boundaries around our readings, we contribute to a more peaceful public reading space that is better for the mental health of everyone. We don't have to *create* for everyone in what we refer to as the collective. One of the helpful approaches I have seen from tarot readers is to define the scenario in the beginning. This reading is about X things and may be helpful to you if you are experiencing X. Even though it is not an individual reading, it can still be beneficial and applicable to groups of listeners because, as the tarot archetypes demonstrate, we all learn in cycles and patterns.

Another useful and widely used tool is "pick a card," where it is up to the listener to use their intuition to choose one message out of a few. I like this approach to reading for the public. Not only does it help to define an audience for the message, it also places some responsibility on the reader to engage in their intuition. This is an essential tool to develop when listening to tarot. It's how we discern what kind of tarot messages are relevant and beneficial. It gets tarot listeners in the active practice of saying no and disengaging with tarot messages they don't find edifying or useful.

As creators in the tarot space, we need to put strong boundaries around our tarot audiences and our work by creating our own spaces (websites, which are digital real estate) so that we can continue to work on our own terms as much as possible. This reduces our vulnerability to algorithm bias, for example. Or to the real threat of losing our communities and livelihood if these apps go down.

For tarot readers, take the time to consider the optimal

conditions for your tarot practice, rather than only which app gives you the most visibility. Resist measuring your work by popularity metrics such as how many followers you have. While large followings can be profitable, they don't necessarily equate to your peace and fulfillment in your work. Nor are they a true measure of the impact your work has on the lives of others. I can point to hundreds of people whose lives I have helped to change through personal readings. My positive influence goes even further than this, but these are clients I know personally. Seeing people happier, freer, more loved, and hopeful means more to me than how many followers I have. Especially if the relationship I have with my followers is transactional, where tarot advice is consumed with little care or investment in me. I see tarot readers lament about this often, but that is the culture of engagement online. I have been able to develop relationships with clients and my community that are patient, kind, and generous. Where my well-being is factored in and respected by the people who choose to work with me. This doesn't happen when we are hyper-focused on numbers instead of connection.

Furthermore, large social media followings come with additional challenges and responsibilities for managing your energy and mental health based on how much access people have to you. You may need time to develop the strength of character and social media management systems that allow that kind of growth to be a positive experience for you.

All of these suggestions are about balancing your practice with your personal needs—they are the daily practice of the Temperance card. Dealing with multiple influences and life changes without being thrown totally off center and disrupting the progress of the beautiful things you are creating in your life. For tarot readers, one of the balancing acts of your practice that you might want to consider is the merit of tarot reading aftercare. Aftercare can be missing or may just feel impossible to create as an individual reader. Once the tarot reading is done, the relationship with the client typically ends there. Out of my empathy I have often given additional time and support to clients through emails and messages but ultimately found that I was overcommitting myself. Repeat clients are an exception because we get to support them over time, but this is still not a community. The resources we get from those readings don't necessarily grow to a point where they can build something sustainable that benefits many. But tarot communities are where that aftercare can take place. For example, I create spaces for people to react to my tarot readings together. Our community holds a weekly series of question prompts so they can think through and discuss together how they feel the Tarot Therapy reading applies to their lives. Sometimes it isn't the communication that is needed for aftercare, but a relaxing movie night together to allow emotional space for the messages of the reading to settle. I could never do all this on my own. This is the wisdom of the Temperance card—the need for others to also give generously. For service-based spiritualists to find the balance in also receiving.

THE HEALING POWER OF
TAROT COMMUNITIES

Though we can adjust and make improvements to our practice as individuals, one of the most beneficial changes we can introduce as the tarot space continues to grow is the creation of tarot communities. When we use the word *community*, sometimes we are thinking of networks we belong to or our social media following—which isn't the same thing. When we talk about spiritual community we mean a space we participate in where care and exchange are reciprocal. Where we understand that our ability to survive the challenges of life (financial, emotional, spiritual, etc.) is dependent on the supportive relationships we build with each other.

Tarot community has supported me in creating a life that is healthy, loving, and increasingly balanced. I am so grateful for the path of rest and pleasure that I have been able to find. I remember a time when I broke down in tears because I was so chronically exhausted but I felt I could not stop doing tarot or I wouldn't be able to afford to live. This is a common feeling for many spirit workers, community healers, and activists. I often see some of the most earnest and giving practitioners offering readings so they can pay rent for the next week. I have definitely been in the same position myself.

When I created my tarot community, it gave us all space to gradually learn healthier ways of healing through the tarot together. I started to see that I was not disposable if

TAROT THERAPY REFLECTION

Shuffle and pull three tarot cards, or journal
and discuss with a therapist or friends:
"WHAT WOULD BE GOOD TAROT
AFTERCARE FOR MYSELF OR OTHERS?"

_____

_____

_____

_____

_____

_____

_____

_____

_____

_____

_____

I couldn't always show up perfectly. When I was sad or hurt or confused, I didn't have to lose my income because I wasn't able to do tarot readings that week. Instead, I was able to be honest and vulnerable with my community. In return they were so willing to love and care for me by holding space for my difficulties and making sure my immediate needs (food and shelter) continued to be met. This was very different from the dynamics of one-on-one client-based work (which I still do).

Like many of the other broken systems in this world, when we simply replicate the business models we see in other industries, it is difficult to make spiritual service work sustainable and financially viable. There are far too many of us as spiritual service workers who are struggling alone when our spiritual communities are essential to our safety. If there were one thing I would want you to take from this discussion of the tarot industry, it would be to not go it alone and to consider whether seeing yourself as a spiritual business—an entrepreneur—is actually limiting your ability to grow your spiritual work and have your needs met.

I would like to see a return to community-based spiritual service where we are all well respected and taken care of. This would be a representation of the Temperance card, where we pour into each other based on connections of reciprocity. Rather than being transactional, where our spiritual work is defined as a paid service only. I would like us to get to a place where our spiritual work under capitalism does not end up compromising our health and physical well-being, but where we can show up for ourselves and others because it's what the heart wants to do.

I have seen the value of a tarot practice that is a mutual exchange. There have been difficult times in my life when my readings for myself have been a complete haze and I have wanted to just stop and give up. But that would leave me stuck and uneasy. I used to persevere through that state, but now I have found that allowing love and support from others in community brings peace and regulation of my fear and anxiety. Importantly, this isn't usually a scheduled and paid-for appointment. With the familiarity and trust built within community any of us can ask "Is someone able to pull a tarot card for me?" or "Can someone pray for me?" This means that financial hardship is not a block to receiving care and support—which has even happened in very practical ways like supporting each other with housing needs. In this way tarot is not limited to advice, but we are able to add to each other in restorative and creative ways.

GOOD PRACTICE IN TAROT

As tarot readers and users, if we don't consider the way we structure our tarot practice, then we don't develop the language or tools of community care and compassionate (self-) accountability. We risk getting stuck in the mindset of consultants and independent spiritual contractors. We definitely make mistakes, have missteps, and miss out on learning better practices as we go along. Our ethics of care

TAROT THERAPY REFLECTION

Shuffle and pull three tarot cards, or journal
and discuss with a therapist or friends:
"WHAT'S THE BEST APPROACH TO
RECEIVING MONEY/RESOURCES FOR ANY
SPIRITUAL WORK I MAY DO?"

_____

_____

_____

_____

_____

_____

_____

_____

_____

_____

_____

_____

and the boundaries of our work need development as we grow and as modern life changes. For example, as a general rule I don't do tarot readings about medical issues. The body and spirit are intricately connected, so that doesn't mean I will never speak about health and well-being. But serious illnesses, like cancer, for example, are not within the purview of a tarot reading with me. That's not because it isn't possible to get useful information about our bodies in the tarot. We can, but I choose not to take on that responsibility. That's my personal boundary. It is easier to develop a good practice and figure out each of our individual boundaries (as reader and as listeners) when we are learning together and from each other's wisdom and experience.

When it comes to experimentation and testing of the Temperance card, let your life be proof. There have to be aspects of your life that express your spirituality in the material world. One of my favorite things was friends and family talking about how much lighter and happier I seemed from the impact of tarot and my spiritual path. How my general disposition had changed. When I do weekly Tarot Therapy readings, people often comment that I'm glowing, and it's not the gold dust highlighter I use! It's because practicing tarot lights me up from within. This is the evidence, this is the proof. Do I do readings for people who accurately describe their circumstances and their choices for their path ahead? Yes. Do I sometimes share publicly prophecies about the political landscape and changes ahead? Yes. All this and more is proof, if the world is looking for it. But my life is the evidence that a tarot practice can blossom and be well balanced.

8

CREATIVITY
Harnessing the Healing
Power of Tarot

The Magician

The Magician

Power, creativity, will,
experimentation, intention,
resourcefulness, action

The Magician of the major arcana stands ready in front of his table with all the items from the four suits of the tarot. Likewise, I hope the chapters of this book have inspired and equipped you to use the tarot creatively for your own healing. As the card that directly follows The Fool's journey, The Magician asks, "What can I do with all that I have picked up along the way?" This is your departure point. How have you been transformed by what you have read? What has this book made you ready for?

Whenever we approach the subject of healing—whether body, mind, or spirit—we need to first determine what obstructs our well-being before we can decide on a remedy. We need a fuller picture of things. By answering the reflection questions in this book, you have been experiencing the diagnostic power of the tarot. The ability to use the tarot to scan and reflect your life as it is currently is just as important a practice as questioning how things could be in the future. Throughout this book I have guided you in doing both. When we use the tarot in this way it becomes a measuring tool that helps us discern the distance between where we are and where we would like our lives to go.

Illustrated holding a wand to the sky in his right hand and pointing downward to the Earth with his left, The Magician represents the transformative action we can take. He symbolizes being ready and willing to use *newly discovered power after a growth experience,* **such as a life lesson, a tarot reading, or finishing this book, for example.** A major theme of the Magician card is experimentation. Even after growing in wisdom and self-awareness, you are not expected to have all the answers. You are not expected to know exactly how to heal yourself at all times. Rather, the wisdom of The Magician is to practice and explore until you find the combination of things that works best for you. **The most important thing is that you have ways to convert the ideas and reflections gained from this book into action.**

CREATING A WAY FORWARD

We want to integrate our learning into intention and direction, so I have a final practice for you to help you continue with Tarot Therapy beyond this book. It is now time to *do* the healing work. You'll need a tarot deck for this. If you don't already have one, I hope now as we come to the end of this book you'll be open to it.

1. Consider yourself as The Magician, honing your power through your tarot deck, just as he holds up his wand. For each of the themes of this book (also listed below as a reminder), I would like you to shuffle a tarot deck you own and pull out one card as a "tarot selfie." This card will represent a snapshot of you *now* in that area of your life. You can make a note of the card and write what you think it means in the table below, on your phone, or in a journal.

2. Take a moment to observe how you feel about this image of yourself and whether it is what you want your life to look like. Now write one word or sentence that either adds to the image on your "tarot selfie" or replaces it if it is not a picture you would like to continue with into the future. If you feel unsure of what you would like to see in that area of your life you could look through the deck and self-select (choose of your own will) another tarot card as your image here.

3. Now with all that you have learned thus far, choose one word or sentence that is an action you will take over the coming weeks to create this new image in your life.

4. As a bonus step, you can shuffle and pull one more tarot card and see whether the plan of action you have made for yourself as The Magician is advised.

To demonstrate, I have done this activity for myself on the theme of purpose (chapter 2):

Chapter Theme	Step 1: Write Down Your Tarot Selfie	Step 2: Comment on or Change Your Tarot Selfie	Step 3: Write an Action You Will Take	Step 4 (Bonus): Suggested Action
PURPOSE	2 of Cups (me supporting others)	10 of Pentacles (a supportive community)	Showing the world my gifts	The Sun (validates my plan)

Chapter Theme	Step 1: Write Down Your Tarot Selfie	Step 2: Comment on or Change Your Tarot Selfie	Step 3: Write an Action You Will Take	Step 4 (Bonus): Suggested Action
LOVE				

PURPOSE			
HEALING			
CHANGE			
TRUTH			
HOPE			

YOU AND YOUR DECK

As you can see from the tarot selfie activity, there are so many creative uses for the tarot. Your deck might be one of the most important tools you use for your healing on a daily basis. Or it could play a minor role as just one tool you use out of many others. Whichever way you choose to use it, let it be a deeply personal practice for you.

Explore which decks you enjoy using most or that give you the clearest answers. Let the traditional meanings of the cards be a helpful structure and starting point for you. But just like any other language, allow the meanings of your cards to also be "local"; develop a dialect with your deck where over time you can have a shorthand for symbols that connect with your specific lived experiences. For example, in my practice, Ace of Wands has become one of the cards that introduces the subject of sex into a tarot reading. Outside of reading the cards in a spread, the evocative imagery can also be used for focusing on a specific theme or doing altar work and rituals. I once bought a deck for the sole purpose of decorating my bedroom wall with my favorite tarot images so that every day I was subconsciously strengthening my intentions to experience those scenes. I even have friends who have used a tarot deck to help plot out the story for their novels. You, as The Magician, get to decide between all the possibilities of what your tarot practice can be.

It is my hope that you will come back to this book over the coming months and years to draw from its guidance and check the compass of your life's direction by revisiting the reflection questions, seeing how your answers change with time. Tarot Therapy is a practice that has helped me find my way through my life challenges and periods of intense difficulty. It has shown me new ways of creating and loving and being in a healthy community with others. I know that it will do the same for you.

TAROT GLOSSARY

COURT CARDS

	Cups	Wands
KING	Emotional Security	Ambition
QUEEN	Nurturing	Personal Power
KNIGHT	Romance	Passion
PAGE	Support	Expansion

	Pentacles	Swords
KING	Dependability	Judgment
QUEEN	Resourcefulness	Discernment
KNIGHT	Steady Progress	Haste
PAGE	First Try	New Ideas

MINOR ARCANA

	CUPS	WANDS
ACE	Heart Opening Receiving Love	Inspiration Initiation
TWO	Love Intimacy	Possibility Expansion
THREE	Friendship Celebration	Optimism Future Planning
FOUR	Disappointment Discontent	Harmony Completion
FIVE	Grief Regret	Contention Opposition
SIX	Nostalgia Innocence	Victory Reward
SEVEN	Imagination Escapism	Standing Your Ground Defense
EIGHT	Release Searching for More	Travel News
NINE	Contentment Being Sociable	Endurance Resilience
TEN	Marriage Family	Burden Breaking Point

	PENTACLES	SWORDS
ACE	Abundance	Truth
	Potential	Clarity
TWO	Change	In Two Minds
	Choice	Stalemate
THREE	Creativity	Heartbreak
	Cooperation	Sorrow
FOUR	Stability	Retreat
	Accumulation	Reflection
FIVE	Neglect	Conflict
	Scarcity	Severance
SIX	Charity	Transition
	Imbalanced Exchange	Moving On
SEVEN	Investment	Deception
	Patience	Avoidance
EIGHT	Diligence	Mental Block
	Hard Work	Stuck
NINE	Independence	Anguish
	Wealth	Anxiety
TEN	Fruition of Goals	Defeat
	Community	Excessive Pain

ABOUT THE AUTHOR

Leona Nichole Black is a passionate educator, well-being advocate, and empathic tarot therapist. She specializes in tarot and cultural studies, engaging popular cultural motifs to explore ways esoteric knowledge can be used to find routes to purposeful living. Leona has been serving as a tarot therapist for over three years, and her practice is founded on the belief that divination through tarot and astrology can deepen our understanding of ourselves through accessing the wisdom of the inner spirit, and that we can use this information for fundamental personal transformations toward a more balanced and empowered life.

Leona is the youngest child of British-Jamaican parents, and she was born and raised in Brixton, South London. An avid foodie, gamer, and film fanatic, you can usually find her under a blanket at home enjoying all three.